Faith in the countryside
transforming communities

Published in 2010 by Rural Ministries

Copyright © Declan Flanagan 2010

ISBN 978-0-9565825-0-8

All rights reserved. No part of this publication may be reproduced or stored or transmitted by any means or in any form, electronic or mechanical, including photocopying, recording, or any information storage and retrieval system without written permission from the Publisher.

Unless indicated otherwise, Scripture quotations are taken from the Holy Bible, New International Version. Copyright © 1973, 1978, 1984 by International Bible Society. Used by permission. All rights reserved.

Design by Adept Design
15 White Hart Street, Aylsham,
Norwich, Norfolk NR11 6HG

Contents

Introduction: Setting the scene   6

1. Context is crucial   11
   Looking
   Listening
   Learning

2. Leadership is essential   26
   Understanding the times
   Knowing what to do
   Possessing a strong determination

3. Build on your strengths not your weaknesses   39
   Present opportunities, not past success or failure
   Assess the resources available
   Do not attempt too much

4. No church is a lost cause but change is never easy   44
   Where are you heading?
   Cul-de-sac or road to growth?
   Flowers in the desert

5. Make buildings work for maximum benefit   60
   Buildings – a blessing or a curse?
   Adaptation not fossilisation
   Raising the standards

6. Church planting needs to be on the agenda   67
   Dealing with objections
   Why plant churches?
   How to plant churches

Endpiece   91

Resources   94

Setting the scene

Every village and market town is likely to have at least one. Some are in good working order while others require tender loving care. A significant number have undergone a change of use and have been converted into residential dwellings. Churches, in spite of rumours to the contrary, continue to prosper in the face of many challenges in rural areas. Each church is different and there are lessons to be learned that may be helpful in other locations.

The last major report on the church in the countryside was published by the Church of England more than twenty years ago. A great deal has changed since then for both Anglican and Free churches. Many people no longer consider that any church could have relevance to their lives. The rites of passage, including births, marriages and deaths, could provide exceptions, along with the possible warm spiritual glow produced by a Christmas service.

Living at times of change

Rural communities and churches have been through very rapid and often uncomfortable changes. In a similar way to the Industrial Revolution in the 18th and 19th centuries that impacted every aspect of daily life, changes in agricultural practice and the growth of information technology are profoundly changing rural communities. The influence of the Internet and the social networking revolution have produced a fundamental shift in both how we communicate and also our understanding of what constitutes a community. How information is found, how business is conducted and how people interact have changed beyond recognition in twenty years.

A new generation has been born which is more comfortable with computers than books. The school bus may be a fact of life, but young people will keep in touch with their friends through text messaging or social networking sites such as Facebook. One in three people in Britain belongs to the Facebook community. Half of these log on daily with the average length of connection being one hour.

Times of rapid change are also periods of great opportunity. Johannes Gutenberg developed the printing press with replaceable and moveable letters in 1440. This led to major advances in the sciences, arts and commerce. Gutenberg's Bible, the first real book to be printed, enabled people to read the Bible in a language they could understand. The Methodist movement, which has now grown to an estimated 70 million adherents worldwide, was particularly influential among all levels of society during the upheaval of the Industrial Revolution.

Is the church being left behind in the face of today's momentous changes? How is it seeking to respond to the challenges of today, and what lessons are being learned?

Negative expectations of rural church life

"A little sleep, a little slumber, a little folding of the hands to rest."
Proverbs 6:10

Signs of hope

At first glance it may appear that the church sleeps while the majority of the population has given up on God. A Tearfund survey in 2007 discovered two thirds of UK adults or 32.2 million people have no connection with church at present. Yet look a little deeper and you discover that not everyone has given in to the modern gods of individual choice and consumerism. The Tearfund survey discovered that as many as three million of those who have stopped going to church or have never attended would be open to an invitation from a relative or friend. There is far more going on in the whole population than is generally appreciated.

Frequently, people have poorly-informed views of the rural church that are unduly negative. They may be unaware that a process of re-envisioning what it really means to be the church of Jesus Christ is under way. The message of the Bible is unchanging, but the context in which we live and witness is never static. In both established and new churches, some fresh models of congregational life are being pioneered in rural areas. God is at work and there are many signs of hope.

The gospel retains the power to change lives and whole communities. One church leader, when asked to describe the purpose of his ministry, promptly responded **'Community transformation – nothing less.'** He had been involved in bringing a divided people together and an innovative youth programme has been developed. The quality of lives has been enhanced as there has been a 'man of peace' at work (Luke 10:6).

'We witness the resurrection in the unfolding of the leaves of each spring.'
Martin Luther

Rural Ministries
PLANTING & GROWING RURAL CHURCHES

Rural Ministries is an evangelical mission agency convinced that the church is God's amazing instrument for bringing life out of death. We are committed to helping rural churches both understand the present and prepare for the future. This takes place as we work alongside more than fifty rural churches located throughout the United Kingdom. Some have existed for many years. Others have been recently planted. Much can be learned from their creativity and commitment. To fulfil our desire to see churches planted and grow we are involved with a wide spectrum of Christian tradition and experience.

As a result of extensive travel and conversations with many church leaders, this publication shows some of the factors that are at work where churches are being planted and renewed. There is information, stories of God at work, and tools that have been effectively used by church leaders. You will find much that is for development and modification in your situation. Each section ends with an Activity. Members of a church leadership team could usefully give time to reading a section individually and then coming together to discuss the implications.

> Strong rural churches are vital to a whole nation. In the past, Holy Spirit-led revivals have commenced in isolated places such as villages in north Wales during 1904 and the Scottish Hebrides in the mid-20th century.
>
> It is easy to forget that Jesus was born in an animal enclosure located in an obscure and out-of-the-way small town. Yet the whole world was changed.

The changing rural landscape – who cares?

With the UK farming industry suffering from rising costs and falling revenues, mega-dairies could see the end of cows grazing outdoors on green grass. Controversial plans for the UK's largest dairy farm of 8,100 cows have been submitted to North Kesteven District Council in Lincolnshire. If the £40 million development goes ahead the cows will be fed on lucerne and crop by-products, bedded on sand, and the slurry will be immediately put through an anaerobic digester that produces power for more than 2,000 homes.

Milking will take place in two 24-hour parlours and the expectation is that at least half a million pints of milk a day will be produced. Animals will apparently be free to roam, but that's only from wall to wall. Risks of disease increases and an outbreak of Foot and Mouth disease would mean slaughtering every single animal. Many smaller dairy farmers will go out of business.

Christians need to be concerned about animal welfare and environmental issues. At local and national level there is a responsibility to declare the earth is not ours to exploit (Psalm 24:1). We are called to be good stewards of what God has entrusted to us (Genesis 1:28 and Genesis 2:15). In the book of Jonah the sin evident among the people of Nineveh negatively impacted the land and animals. Repentance was called for and God's concern for people and cattle is expressed (Jonah 4:11). The creation waits in eager expectation for the sons of God to be revealed (Romans 8:19).

1. Context is crucial

For many urban and suburban dwellers, expectations of life in a rural area bear little resemblance to the reality. The Estate Agents' particulars will proclaim the virtues of properties in sought-after locations, enhanced by clean air, peace and quiet – and all with spectacular views. A1 condition could mean the A1 road runs through your garden! The agent's idea of a village could mean one of two things. Either that a school, shop and pub continues to exist or that the place is largely deserted. Whether it is the potential house purchaser or a church seeking to develop, a more thorough investigation is required.

With the decline in the number of people working in agriculture to less than 2% of the UK population, the composition of rural areas is significantly different from that of twenty years ago. Farm workers are now outnumbered seven to one by National Trust members. Rural life has previously changed relatively slowly, but recent changes have been much more dramatic.

The church is often seen as a bastion of conservatism and the preserver of tradition. It does not find it easy to respond to changes in society. No longer can we expect people to fit into the church's rhythms and expectations. Such rhythms reflect a long-lost vision of life lived within an agriculturally-dominated environment that may no longer exist. The sad truth is that where a church is more in love with its collective culture than with God and those he has made, it may be subject to decline and eventual closure. No church has a God-given right to exist forever. The seven churches in Revelation 2-3 illustrate this.

In order to appreciate the unique circumstances relating to a particular church context, understanding must be sought through a careful process of **looking, listening** and **learning**. In the early days of an overseas missionary assignment, this is what the new missionary will spend considerable time doing. The requirement is no less in the UK where each village and church has its own particular history, values and stories.

On nine occasions in the gospels, Jesus encourages people to 'look'. Three times he speaks of the importance of 'listening', and the necessity of hearing is emphasised in the seed parables of Matthew 13. The invitation of the Lord to draw on resources that he alone may provide remains the same: *'Are you tired? Worn out? Burned out on religion? Come to me. Get away with me and you'll recover your life. I'll show you how to take a real rest. Walk with me and work with me – watch how I do it. Learn the unforced rhythms of grace. I won't lay anything heavy or ill-fitting on you. Keep company with me and you'll learn to live freely and lightly'* (Matthew 11:29-30 *The Message*).

Looking

There is no uniformity to rural Britain and generalisations are dangerous. A village in the Cotswolds will be very different from one in Northumberland. Intensive food production in parts of Kent will be vastly different from the challenges of securing a living from rearing sheep in mid Wales. Making a home in an affluent dormitory village outside the M25 where cricket is played on the green is a world away from the isolation of coastal areas in Cumbria

So what *is* a rural area? Since 2004, the Department of the Environment, Food and Rural Affairs has been defining rural areas as those having population densities that are either 'less sparse' or 'sparse'. Accessibility to surrounding towns, cities and places of employment are significant factors. Most of us tend to understand places as being either city, suburban, town, rural and outer rural. Outer rural areas contain 1.4% of the population and will be further from major settlements. It is generally accepted that a rural settlement will consist of less than 10,000 people. This will include some market towns. In some outer rural areas, the market town and its churches will seem a world away from hamlets with less than 100 inhabitants.

The idealised rural community, where most people work on the land and nothing much happens very quickly, may be appropriate for a television series like 'Lark Rise to Candleford'. But the present reality is very different. Rural communities are complex places. Look beyond the roses and wisteria and you discover a very diverse group of people belonging to different subcultures and networks. These are the people with whom the rural church must connect. In many places, it is possible to discover at least some of the following groups which define the local context.

Villagers

Long-stay residents may have been born and bred in the village and have associations going back several generations. Farmers are now likely to have few employees, and many have diversified into new areas such as tourism. Villagers may have previously found work on the land or in local industries. But the increase in the industrialised production of livestock, fish, poultry and crops has meant a reduction in available local work. These villagers usually have a strong attachment to a place or church and they often mix socially with others who have been resident for many years.

Incomers

The movement from town to country has been a marked feature during the past twenty years. Rural Britain is an increasingly popular place in which to live. An estimated one million people have relocated to the country in the last ten years. Such movements inevitably lead to consequences for the long-stay residents, especially if incomers have

13

an idealised view of what their escape to the country should look like.

Incomers may have chosen to move to the country for lifestyle reasons. Tranquillity, better schools, lower crime rates and a pleasant environment are all on their wish list. Some will have come to retire, but the majority of incomers are between 30 and 50 years old. Others have relocated as a result of changes in employment or for family reasons.

Criticisms of incomers often include responsibility for increases in house prices, taking jobs from villagers, or a commuting lifestyle that contributes little to the local economy. Questions of access to land, mud and slurry on roads, and plans to sell agricultural land for development will certainly disturb the apparent local peace.

Country retreaters

Frequently living in barred and gated modern houses or modernised rustic properties, with at least one 4x4 vehicle parked on the driveway, these high achievers may be pleased to enjoy their isolation while continuing their social networks elsewhere. Architects and expensive designers will have been paid to create bespoke homes with style. Others will be owners of a second home that may be rented for income or used for occasional visits.

Migrant workers

The seasonal nature of agriculture and tourism brings an influx of workers who are far from home, poorly paid and have no job security. Often unseen by the majority, up to 120,000 arrive annually from countries that have recently joined the European Union. There is a seasonal trend, with September as the peak for new registrations. Some will be Christians seeking friendship and fellowship.

For the church, migrant workers – frequently ignored or received with hostility – the words of Jesus in Matthew 25:35 are appropriate:

'I was hungry and you gave me something to eat, I was thirsty and you gave me something to drink, I was a stranger and you invited me in.'

The poor

Two recent studies highlighted the extent of rural poverty. The Commission for Rural Communities reports that nearly a million rural households are living below the poverty threshold (set at an annual income of £16,492 in 2008). These people number the size of the Birmingham conurbation, but scattered throughout the UK.

The Rural Services Network warns that many rural areas lack affordable housing, training opportunities for the young, and financial support to care for an ageing population. Many young people have to relocate for higher education or employment or to find affordable housing. Increases in fuel costs have a serious impact on those living in outer rural areas who have to travel long distances just to get basic services.

In our prayers and actions, we should join the Psalmist in asking the Lord to 'Defend the cause of the weak and fatherless; maintain the rights of the poor and oppressed' (Psalm 82:3).

More TV vicar?

The parish of St Mary Magdalene, Lundwood near Barnsley, South Yorkshire is situated in one of the poorest parts of the UK. It is far from the rural idyll.

In 2005, the Vicar, Rev James McCaskill, featured in the Channel 4 fly-on-the-wall documentary 'Priest Idol'. Lundwood village is strung out along a main road. Where verges exist, they are sprinkled with litter. Some 20% of adults are dependent on benefits. The population of 3,000 has seen economic and social decline since three coalmines closed, the last in 1991. Press reports speak of third generation unemployment, truancy, heroin addiction, boarded-up houses and vandalised properties.

Plans are in place to develop a corner of the church gardens into a Community Garden Allotment. This will offer a programme for disaffected young people, and provide fresh produce to the Miner's Lamp Café in the Village Life Centre once it is built. This is designed to replace the Church Hall that was burnt down in 2006.

The elderly

As many rural young people have to relocate, the average age of the remaining population rises. It is now on average three years higher than that of residents in urban areas.

Today, among those living in the countryside are more than 2.3 million over the age of 60. This growing segment of the population provides excellent opportunities for Christians to both serve and befriend. God is not ageist and a caring church will not neglect the practical and spiritual needs of the elderly. We must seek many more who will 'still bear fruit in old age, they will stay fresh and green' (Psalm 92:14).

Homeworkers

Around a fifth of those living in rural Britain now run a business from their home. According to the insurer NFU Mutual, the recent recession has created a new breed of 'country-preneurs', as some living away from the towns set up enterprises in their own living space. For those who previously have worked with other people, isolation becomes a problem. Creative new opportunities could develop for the church to bring people together.

Tourists

Walking is the most popular leisure activity in Britain. For many, the countryside is a place to visit and discover how other people live. Lunch at the local pub – if it still exists – and possibly a peep inside the church – if it is open – could be on their agenda.

Holidays in the past were 'holy days', times for worship, play and refreshment. Some churches in tourist areas are taking the initiative in inviting people to enjoy a day marked by joy, wonder, simplicity and the opportunity to meet those from very different lifestyles. Where churches are open, the provision of good quality, relevant literature is most helpful. It is regrettable when all the attention is given to the architectural merit of the building and nothing is communicated about the Lord who is to be worshipped.

Contexts change over a period of time, sometimes slowly but occasionally quite dramatically. New and different people may come to live in an area. Looking to observe carefully who lives within the proximity of a church is a vital starting point.

Listening

Listening locally

Every hamlet, village and small town has a story to tell. Stories involving people, personalities and significant events. Long-term residents will certainly have more in their memory banks than incomers. As the past shapes the present, knowing these stories is vital. Sometimes, a story will go back generations, and distinguishing fact from fiction may prove difficult. Taking time to listen in order to appreciate the particular local factors builds a great appreciation of the character of a community. It can also help avoid potential pitfalls.

As the process of listening develops, you quickly discover that people meet and speak together in a variety of social contexts. If there is a school, parents will meet outside its gates. Teenagers may travel together on the school bus to the nearest town. Any remaining village shops usually provide all the local gossip anyone could ever desire. Where there are sporting activities, other clubs or places of employment, people come together. Farmers will have created their own networks, and a visit to the local market is the time not only to buy and sell but also to discuss the latest local or farming issues. Each social network will have its own stories and set of values.

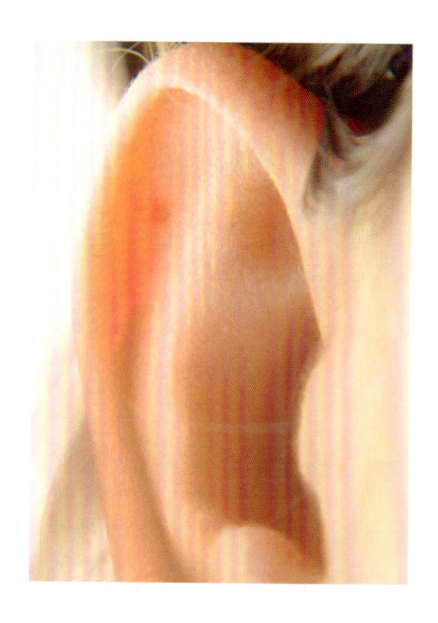

Where a church community has become largely static and insular, it becomes progressively detached from other crucial networks. There may be little listening to people outside the church, and internal issues may become the regular topics of conversation. A small church is unlikely to have people involved in every social grouping, but low levels of participation are a danger sign. And some local networks may prove impenetrable.

Listening well

Carlton Colville Methodist Church, near Lowestoft, Suffolk, sought assistance from Christian Research and the University of East Anglia to discover how their church could more effectively serve their community. New homes were being built and the church wanted local residents to lead fulfilling lives by providing facilities to meet their physical and social needs as well as their spiritual needs.

Results from over 900 completed questionnaires indicated that the strongest demand among school pupils aged 15-18 was for a fitness centre (30%) and a café/coffee shop. Many female respondents requested a place for art and craft activities. There was also strong support for a community cinema.

66% of respondents seemed to prefer weekday evenings as free time for activities, while weekends were less popular than weekdays. 7% had some form of physical disability and have asked for special consideration such as easy access. 65% of people do not follow any religious faith. Of those who follow a religious faith 25% of respondents visit places of worship outside Carlton Colville.

The church is now intending to develop relevant programmes and facilities based on the survey results. The church website contains a full report and includes the questionnaire used. www.carltoncolvillemethodistchurch.org

> The further away the culture you are trying to reach is from the dominant culture in the church, the longer it will take for you to understand what is going on.

Christians are not only called to proclaim good news but to *be* good news within their communities. This cannot adequately be done from a distance. A congregation consisting of people who travel from other villages or towns will have difficulty in establishing links with local residents.

Local involvement and a willingness to listen may point to new directions for a church.

Listening in the church

As well as listening to discover more about the immediate context, it is vital to listen to those who are already involved with the church. Each church will have its own particular stories, and every one will have developed its own corporate personality. Each person comes with their own hopes and expectations. Although church leaders may assume that their own beliefs and patterns of life have been influenced by Christian teaching, family factors and past experiences are not inconsequential. Accepted church traditions may have arisen for unknown reasons and these are not quickly overturned. Failure to listen carefully to those in the church often leads to unnecessary tension and conflict.

Listening to God

The third element of listening is often the most neglected. Taking time to listen and speak with God in prayer brings access to the resources that only he possesses. The first reaction to a growing awareness of the challenges of countryside ministry is often to call a meeting, make a plan or write a report. Solutions driven by human endeavour change very little, and they quickly exhaust enthusiastic people.

When we are not talking and listening to God, we are missing a golden opportunity to draw closer to him, to get to know him better, and to let him know that we need his help. Jesus told his disciples, 'Apart from me you can do nothing' (John 15:5). As we seek direction for the church, the Lord has promised, 'My sheep listen to my voice; I know them, and they follow me' (John 10:27).

Four crucial questions

When it comes to listening to God, how do we know if we are hearing from him? Ask:

1. Is it consistent with what God has already said in the Bible?
2. Would Jesus be prepared to put his name to this?
3. Does this fit God's overall plan for your life or church?
4. Does this solution honour God?

Learning

The time to learn is not just childhood or the early stages of our Christian discipleship. We need a greater emphasis on lifelong learning. The rapid pace of change in rural communities means that keeping up with what is going on is a constant necessity. Old certainties are less certain. Previous patterns of church life may no longer be appropriate. How the church has previously engaged in mission may require examination and alteration. All this can seem threatening and our natural reaction is to maintain a 'business as usual' attitude.

Children are more adaptable than adults. They do not have so many past experiences to rely on and so they do not quickly dismiss new opportunities. Jesus said, 'I tell you the truth, anyone who will not receive the kingdom of God like a little child will never enter it' (Mark 10:15).

Humility is essential if churches are to acknowledge present difficulties and realise that asking for outside help may be necessary. Within the work of Rural Ministries, our first contact with a church often comes though a telephone call that commences, 'We are unsure of where to begin, but perhaps you could help?'

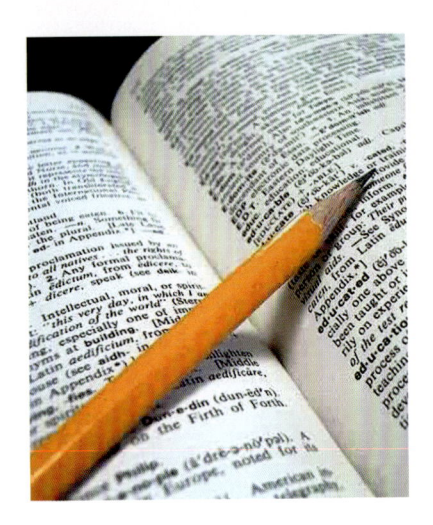

Keeping up with appropriate courses, books, conferences and training events will help promote greater understanding, as will listening to and learning from other local churches in your area that are growing. Isolation is dangerous and an involvement with the wider church is most helpful.

Summary

Appreciating that context is crucial is the first lesson to be learned concerning faith in the countryside. This starting point requires careful looking, listening and learning.

The realities of life and ministry in rural Cumbria

Bootle is located in the Lake District National Park, and is close to the Irish Sea coast. At the 2001 census, it had a population of 745.

Scratch beneath the surface and you soon realise the difficulties of life in a remote place, 28 miles from a medium-sized town. We do not have many of the facilities that are available in larger communities. The only access to a library demands a 20-minute car journey or waiting for the monthly visit of the mobile library with its limited stock and no additional facilities. The village school has only about 20 pupils.

We have no bus service and the nearest train station, with a very limited service, is two miles away. Substantial travel is needed to attend any but the smallest local gatherings and to visit the sick or go to hospital. This can involve at best a 56-mile round trip – and at worst over 200 miles. Fortunately our population seems relatively healthy!

Most people in Bootle have several functions. A farmer is a retained fireman; the Post Office clerk is a special constable; the local carpenter is also the undertaker. We only have a limited number willing to serve on village committees and to take on church roles.

Church ministry in an area as remote as ours involves the paradox of a lot of travel and a lot of staying in one place. The latter means being available to villagers – to be known as available and able to be found when needed. It is difficult to visit people at work. The farmer, for example, cannot easily leave the farm, nor is it very convenient to talk in a tractor cab or in a sheep pen. Even a home visit needs an appointment lest you drive or walk miles to find no one at home.

As for older folk in the village, most are self-sufficient. But they value the social contact of events like coffee mornings, light lunches and so on. We seek opportunities for churchgoers to meet those who do not come to services; to offer social, spiritual, and in some cases physical, care. But such meetings are the only contact many people have with the church.

In a village this size, everybody knows who you are, what you do, and what they *think* you are trying to do! People are so familiar with these things that it is difficult to really share the gospel.

Young people also have difficulties meeting other Christian youngsters. At present, there are only three Christian teenagers in the village. Do their parents make a 20-mile round trip to take them to the nearest small town where there is a youth club? Or do we hold a youth club for just three?

Our remote location means access to Christian counselling and other forms of spiritual help is very limited. We lack the stimulus of interaction with other Christians and churches. However much the minister is a general practitioner, there is no time to be a specialist. Our needs are great, and we ask how can they be met? Only by serious prayer, perseverance and dependence upon the Lord

James Thomas is Minister of Bootle Evangelical Church, Cumbria
www.bootlechapel.org.uk

Fact file

- In England and Wales, 1 person in 5 lives in a rural area. This totals around 12 million people.
- Wales (36%) has the highest proportion of those living in rural areas compared with the English regions, where the South West has the highest proportional rural population (34%), followed by the East (31%).
- Of rural households, 44% comprise a married couple. This is 9% higher than in urban areas.
- The rural population aged 65 and over is 18%, compared with 15% in urban areas.
- Of the rural population, 8 in 10 describe themselves as Christian.
- Fewer than 5% of rural people work in agriculture, forestry or fishing.
- In rural areas, 14% of working people work at or mainly from home.

Source: Office of National Statistics 2005

- Of 15-29 year-olds, 190,000 left the countryside in 2008. They moved for educational reasons, a dearth of affordable housing, a lack of modern services including fast Internet access, and to find employment.
- Of rural 16-24 year-olds, 40% are unemployed.

Source: Report on The State of the Countryside, Stuart Burgess, Government Rural Advocate

- The total number of rural churches is two-thirds that of urban churches (urban 22,080 and rural 15,421).
- The average urban congregational size is 116 with average rural congregations being 39.

Source: English Church Census 2005

Activity One

Exploring your context: Getting started

Each church is a combination of many factors. These include history, context, personality, and vision. On your own, seek to briefly answer the questions below. Then in a larger group share your observations. In particular, look for repeated statements as these will be indicators of substantial agreement.

1. Choose one word to sum up your village and then do the same thing for your church.
2. Where has your church come from? (Your history) What have been three significant events?
3. Where is it? (your context)
4. What is it? (your personality)
5. What are you called to become? (your vision)
6. What do people in your community think of your church?
7. What have been the biggest challenges faced by the church during the past three years?
8. Could your church be less than one generation from extinction?

Activity Two

Exploring your context: Digging deeper

> Bring together a group prepared to look more closely at both the church and community. Each group member should explore the answers to one question below before coming together to share their findings.

Knowing the church

1. Who attends church here?

Look at Sundays, midweek, age and gender profiles. What are the dominant age groups in the congregation? What were the dominant groups 10 and 20 years ago? How does the present age range compare to that of your surrounding community? How long have people been involved in the church? What contributions do they make?

2. Who lives where?

Seek to identify on a map the locations of those involved in the church. How far are people travelling? What transport do they use? What is the potential geographical sphere of influence of the church?

3. Who works where?

Mark on a map the work place locations of those involved in your church.

Knowing your community

1. Who lives here?

What can you find out about those living in your locality? Where possible, discover information relating to age, housing, education, health, mobility and employment and other factors.

Census data and websites such as www.upmystreet.com are useful. Visit your nearest library and council offices. Talk to local Councillors. Discover more about local history. Identify the main forms and places of employment in your area.

Look back in this chapter at the section seeking to identify groups of people who may live in your area.

- What groups do you observe?
- What groups may be missing from those described?

2. Who meets where?

Identify meeting places of various groups within your locality and seek to discover where people in the church meet apart from church buildings.

3. Looking at both church and community

When each member of the group has reported their findings, explore:

1. What have you discovered about the church and community?
2. Did anything you have found either shock or surprise you?
3. How representative is the church of the surrounding community?
4. Do you think there is a significant gap between the dominant culture of the church and the local community? Is there any connection between what those in the church talk about and what concerns local people?
5. What changes would make a significant difference to the link between church and community?
6. How could you communicate some of your findings with others in the church?

Activity Three
Community survey

Devise a short questionnaire using your own questions or some of those listed below and seek to engage people in conversation. This could come through a visitation programme where you inform homes in advance that you will be calling.

1. How long have you lived in this area?
2. How would you describe this area?
3. What is the best thing about living here?
4. Is there anything you particularly dislike about living here?
5. Do you follow a particular faith?
6. Have you ever visited any of the churches in the area?
7. Do you think the church has anything to offer?
8. When this survey is complete we will publish the results. Would you like a copy?

2. Leadership is essential

Regular preaching, teaching, prayer, training, pastoral care, administration and visitation are all important. But without leadership any church will struggle. A growing number of ever-pressing demands will mean there is little energy to explore what the church of tomorrow should or might look like.

In studies of growing churches throughout the world, a common factor found is the presence of capable leadership. Following a study based on more than 1,000 churches in 32 countries, Christian Schwarz, author of *Natural Church Development*, wrote that empowering leadership was one of the characteristics common to healthy churches. 'Leaders of growing churches concentrate on empowering other Christians for ministry. They do not use lay workers as helpers in attaining their own goals and fulfilling their own visions. Rather, they invert the pyramid of authority so that the leader assists Christians to attain the spiritual potential God has for them. These pastors equip, support, motivate and mentor individuals, enabling them to become all that God wants them to be.'

Throughout the Bible, we observe that true leaders are those who walk closely with God. This requires a strong and developing faith. You will be confident that, if God has called you to a position of leadership, he will provide you with the resources you need. All godly leaders are very aware of their own shortcomings. Paul writes at a time when his leadership is being criticised that 'For Christ's sake, I delight in weaknesses, in insults, in hardships, in persecutions, in difficulties. For when I am weak, then I am strong' (2 Corinthians 12:10).

Located in 1 Samuel 22 is an account of how David's army grew from a handful of distressed, indebted and discontented stragglers in the cave of Adullam to a mighty fighting force. These were not people used to wielding power or exercising influence. A major transformation took place that resulted in a well-disciplined and united team, with a singular purpose, led by gifted emerging leaders, seeking to serve God and do his will. Crucial to David's team was a group known as the men of Issachar (1 Chronicles 12:32). They possessed the following three essential qualities of leaders at any period of history.

Understanding the times

Joining with David were not the most apparently gifted, but those with accurate perceptions and penetrating analysis. They understood that their generation was at a crossroads and had to decide for or against God.

Today, gaining understanding requires spiritual perception and ongoing education as well as considerable patience. Some who have lived in city or suburban situations will find moving to a rural area requires a cross-cultural mindset. Time and a willingness to develop understanding are essential. Logical presentation of reasons to make a particular change in a rural church may fall on deaf ears. Country people may approach issues from a much more personal perspective, that of their own identity and family history.

Knowing what to do

Understanding must lead to action. It is possible to be caught up in the paralysis of analysis to such an extent that nothing is actually done. The reality of indecision is that it is a decision not to make a decision. Most good decisions will be based on the patient work of listening, considering options and resolving what to do. Uncertain times need leaders of real strength and character who know what to do for the right reasons.

In order to be a leader with influence, the quality of relationships is essential. Rural people tend to know each other, and the way in which a minister relates to everyone is noticed. There is no place to hide in a village. Regularly perplexing spiritual, moral and ethical issues will have to be faced. Indiscreet comments or breaches in confidentiality erode trust and produce major complications. Discovering in the context of prayer how to handle a particular situation, and then having the courage to take the necessary action will be a mark of effective leadership.

The parable of the globes and pears

The owner of a large house particularly appreciated the way his gardener sculptured the top of his boxwood hedging into globes. On one occasion while the gardener had been in hospital for heart surgery, some temporary help had changed the shapes of hedge from globes to pears. The man was convinced that traditional globe shapes were out of fashion and a more contemporary look would attract new visitors. On returning to work to see his hedge, the regular gardener turned the air blue with his swearing. He quickly located the visiting gardener and cried, 'It will take years to change the shape of these trees, because **you can only change the tree to the degree it has grown.**'

Possessing a strong determination

Along with other volunteers who joined David's army (1 Chronicles 12:38), the men of Issachar came together with an enthusiasm and passion that was contagious. Most advances of the kingdom of God will be opposed, and a leader must not be deflected by criticism. A humble attitude linked with a positive outlook will gain the support of the vast majority.

Through the Chronicler's narrative you discover additional qualities of capable leaders. They possessed a radical dependence on a great God (verse 18) and an ability to work together and enjoy each other's company (verse 39).

Many rural churches stand at a crossroads with the world watching. Like David's army, we may feel threatened and outnumbered, weak in resources. We pray that those who are watching will be aware that God is unchanging and capable of doing amazing and unimagined things that will bring him glory. For that to take place, godly leadership in the church is essential.

Regrettably many attitudes to paid or stipendiary ministry in the countryside are frequently negative. Some ministers may regard it as a stepping stone to greater things elsewhere. Where success in church is often measured by numbers attending, moving on to larger congregations will be expected of the young and capable. This clearly works against the time required to know, understand and gain the respect of a particular community. Others regard rural ministry as the place to spend a more leisurely period before retirement. While not underestimating the value of experienced people in ministry, it has been good to see an increase in some young leaders prepared to go and stay in some of the most neglected places in Britain.

Those who choose to worship locally will often come from a variety of church backgrounds, with differing theologies and expectations. This results in many rural churches being more diverse than those in urban or suburban settings. So ministry in rural areas is demanding, complex and multi-faceted.

Why I still minister on Skye

Ten years ago, God clearly called me to Staffin and Kilmuir on the Scottish Isle of Skye, a parish of only 900 people. In grappling with that call I had certain fears to overcome. There was the fear that the parish was so small and so remote that it would be limiting in terms of ministry opportunities. There was also the fact that my own roots are in north Skye. While I relished the prospect of serving God in a place I love dearly, I feared the possibility of being a prophet without honour in his own country. God has answered these fears wonderfully and has given me a ministry here which is both varied and challenging.

In our worshipping congregation of around 90, I have found a sense of community that is rare in larger, more gathered congregations. There is a strong bond between the congregation and me. This has enabled me, along with the other elders, to lead the congregation relatively quickly in developing our style of worship, our fellowship and outreach.

I am less encumbered with regular ministry demands that overwhelm many of my city colleagues. This has been a great advantage, allowing me to give myself to the core tasks of preaching, teaching and prayer. The size of the congregation has meant that it has been possible to enjoy a ministry that is both more intensive and extensive. Intensively, I can take time to mentor future leaders, disciple new Christians and visit members systematically. The longer I have been here, the greater a sense of shared theological outlook there has been. Extensively, I have been able to involve myself in wider ministries including a Scottish church planting initiative and an overseas mission partnership.

My reading of the Old Testament especially leads me to believe that commitment to place, to land and community is important. In the modern world we suffer from the condition of hyper-mobility leading to the feeling that every relationship is temporary. A congregation with roots pastored by a minister committed to people and place can be a sign of the kingdom of God.

God has been good to us here. He is building a team which I pray will partner Christ's church in places where it is weaker. Unless God has other plans, I hope to stay around to see that happen!

Ivor Macdonald is the Church of Scotland Minister at Staffin and Kilmuir on Skye

Uncomfortable truths

The time has come to be honest and realistic about paid ministry in the future. The past twenty years have seen many old models of ministry either breaking down or in the process of doing so. Many churches would like and expect to have their own omnipresent and multi-talented spiritual leader, but this is no longer possible. Increasingly the effective rural church leader will be someone who does not attempt to do everything, but is capable of coming alongside and enabling others. The expectations of that role, including marrying and burying well, will not be underestimated, but such leaders will be comfortable in a variety of situations.

Developing Leaders

A survey conducted by the Centre for Theology and Land in the USA asked 100 rural churches described as exemplary, what factors contributed to their vitality? Of those 100 surveyed, 88 agreed that indispensable to the energy and drive of their congregation was the development of lay leadership. This was a significant 39% higher than the next contributing factor.

Financial constraints and a pension funding crisis are quickly having a major impact on paid ministry in the Church of England. It costs in excess of £40,000 per annum for an Anglican stipendiary minister. Growing financial pressures have resulted in the expectation that as many as one in ten paid clergy will be lost in the next five years.

A similar funding crisis is evident in Free churches. Adequately funding a minister and any family is a constant challenge. Many Free Church ministers in the countryside are earning appreciably less than the national average weekly wage. The reality is that some are dependent for survival on social security benefits or a working spouse. Financial pressures often place an unacceptable burden on those who are willing to serve but unlikely to complain.

Looking ahead

Future patterns of ministry are likely to include more couples who are able to survive on one income or have other paid employment. Acts 18:2-4 records Paul's willingness to work as a tentmaker while at Corinth. I doubt this was his preferred option, but was right in that context. There are many ministers who indicate they seem to have two full time jobs and this presents particular pressures of which a church should be aware. And of course, part-time work is not easy to find in some parts of the country or for some age groups.

Ministry will also be provided by those who will have had other careers and may not require a full stipend. Within the Church of England, there are nearly 2,000 non-stipendiary ministers. This compares with a steadily diminishing number of stipendiary clergy, anticipated to dip below 9,000 within the next three years. The increased emphasis on training the laity has produced churches that are much less dependent on the clergy with more local people becoming actively involved.

In parts of the world where churches are growing most rapidly, the emphasis on lay ministry is very evident. Teams where different gifts are apparent enable a greater scope for ministry.

Another pattern that is likely to increase is that of ministers being involved in more than one church. This has been more readily accepted in the Church of England than among Free churches. It will be necessary to accept team ministries serving several churches or that sharing a minister will be better than not having one at all.

It is not easy to be a rural minister today. Because of the multiple demands upon those who are willing, it is also potentially dangerous. There is often a greater freedom for the minister to make a personal choice about the use of time. The downside may be a lack of order to the working day and week. In turn, this may lead towards laziness, spiritual indiscipline and following the route of least resistance. For those prepared to show initiative, there will be dangers associated with disturbing the status quo and being prone to personal impatience. Well-conducted appraisals will help to avoid the lack of accountability and other dangers.

If rural Britain is to have healthy churches, they will require men and women who possess character and integrity and who are prepared to understand the resources, problems and needs of rural people, for the sake of Jesus Christ.

Summary

The second lesson concerning faith in the countryside is that good leadership is essential. Healthy churches have leaders who understand the times, know what to do and possess strong determination.

Three churches – one Baptist minister

In 2003, I was invited to pastor a group of three Baptist churches in rural Lincolnshire. This was the first time that I had led multiple churches and I had no idea how to go about it.

When I arrived, two of the churches only had evening services and the third was closed. The first step was to encourage one of the churches to move its service to a morning. The next was to re-open the closed church with a monthly afternoon service, so that at least I could take all the services in all the churches. If a group of churches join together, they have to be willing to compromise and make changes where necessary to accommodate one minister.

The next challenge was trying to satisfy each centre as if I was their full-time minister, and inevitably there are issues. The manse can only be in one village and it is natural that it is *there* where you become best known and most involved. The other churches can easily feel that they came second or third in the pecking order and sadly, that is almost inevitable. Therefore time management is a great challenge.

It soon became obvious that each of the three churches had their own identity, churchmanship, traditions and personalities. It was not possible to treat any of the three services in the same way, or to simply repeat sermons, as each church was in a different place spiritually. It is most important to bear that in mind at all times and I personally feel that it is great to have different styles in different locations as it may help meet differing needs. It also offers the opportunity for members of one church to support the other churches and take part in what they have to offer.

David Hughes is Minister at Morton, Dyke and Haconby Baptist Churches, Lincolnshire

Top 10 requirements for a rural church leader:

1. Sure of a calling rather than seeking a career.
2. Able to relate the Bible to people's lives.
3. Belief that through prayer, God works.
4. Capable of shaping the local context rather than being shaped by it.
5. Prepared to listen, visit, seek understanding and draw people together.
6. Looks forward to the major festivals of Christmas, Easter and Harvest and creatively arranges special initiatives and invitations.
7. Unwilling to be a spectator in the community.
8. Desire to serve as chaplain to the whole community, not just the church.
9. Comfortable while speaking about farming, sport, politics or nonsense.
10. In possession of a pair of mucky wellington boots and possibly a dog.

Cardboard congregation

Reverend Frederick William Densham, aged and eccentric Rector of St Bartholomew's Church in Warleggan, on the edge of Bodmin Moor, Cornwall, walks the path alongside the church to which he was appointed in 1931 at the age of 61

Frederick Densham's autocratic style soon led him into conflict with the Parochial Church Council over styles of service and his desire to remove the church organ. This instrument had been bought by public subscription and was a war memorial. He became a vegetarian, a very alien concept in a remote farming community such as Warleggan. Previously, a popular church event had been the rook and pigeon shoot – but no more! Often attendance at services dwindled to the Rector alone, though he meticulously detailed all the services and thereby fulfilled the conditions of his tenure. Of his parishioners, he said 'They all come to me in the end. I conduct their funerals. They won't come to church on their feet, but they come in their black carriages.'

It was rumoured that in lieu of a congregation he would sometimes prop up cardboard shapes of parishioners in the pews. Week after week as the service reached its conclusion, he would note poignantly in the register, 'No fog, no wind, no rain, no congregation.' As the years went by he grew more eccentric, more reclusive and the rectory was fortified against intruders and casual visitors.

Despite his wish to be buried in the 'Garden of Remembrance' he had created within the Rectory grounds, his body was cremated and his ashes scattered in the public garden of remembrance in Plymouth.

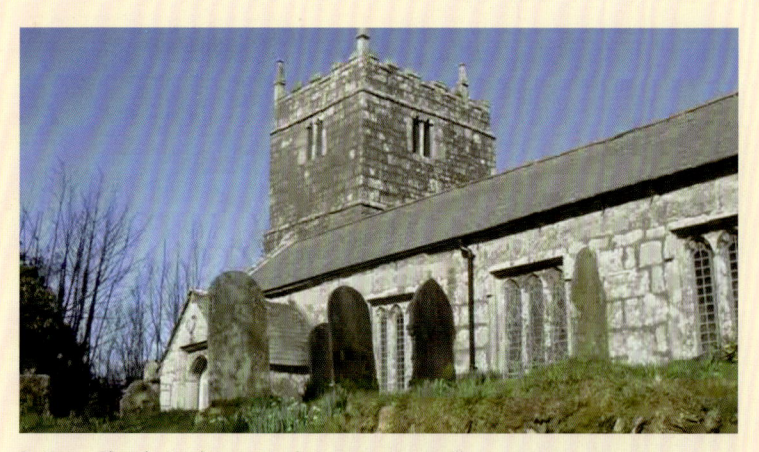

St James Church, Warleggan, Bodmin Moor, Cornwall

Activity One
Do what he failed to do

1. Read again the section on the 'Cardboard Congregation', and discuss what went wrong for Rev Fredrick Densham.
2. What can you learn that would be helpful in your situation?

Activity Two
Check out whether you are leading or following

> If you are a church leader, think about yourself and your fellow church leaders. Use the questions below to evaluate your current approach to leadership. You could invite others in the church to also participate in this activity. Your discussions are not designed to apportion blame but to point to some new directions.

Leaders understand the times

1. Would you agree with the statement that 'If you are a church leader, the future is in your hands'?
2. How could you become more aware of the realities of life for those in your church and community?
3. Do you think your church is for the present day 'fit for purpose'?

Leaders know what to do

1. When you meet together, what priority does seeking God for his wisdom and strength have?
2. How much of your time do you spend shaping the future and how much maintaining the present?
3. Have you ever asked what should you stop doing?

Leaders possess a strong determination

1. As you read the gospels you realise how purposeful and focused Jesus was during his three years of ministry. Have you sunk into a survival routine? What can you do to refocus attention on doing two things well rather than many things badly?
2. What are you doing to communicate and keep communicating the direction of travel for the church? Are you able to say: 'This year we will concentrate on the following…'?

3. How do you tend to react when resistance is encountered? How do you encourage each other to persevere under pressure?

4. Do you share the conviction that growth is from the Lord but we must play our part? See 1 Corinthians 3:6-9.

5. Identify and thank God for people who have effectively modelled Christian leadership.

Activity Three
Take the mirror test

> Personal integrity is vital for church leaders especially in a village where everything that moves is noticed by somebody.

Each day as you look in the mirror, ask whether the person you see is the kind of person you want to be, respect and believe in. Where there is a divide between your public and private lives, increasingly you will be unable to manage the divide. Especially under pressure, the cracks will start to appear and the truth will come out.

Jesus said, 'There is nothing hidden that will not be disclosed, and nothing concealed that will not be known or brought out into the open' (Luke 8:17).

3. Build on your strengths not your weaknesses

Words of introduction at the start of the letters to the seven churches in Revelation 2-3 are relevant to every church today. To each church, the Lord says 'I know your...' His knowledge is complete and always accurate. His grace does not drive us to do more and more and exhaust ourselves in the process.

The small church frequently suffers from a crisis of identity. It may also be prone to a sense of inferiority on hearing about the programmes existing in larger churches. 'Why would anyone want to come to *us*?' is a frequent question.

> Success in a small church is notoriously difficult to measure. Levels of participation and involvement are good starting points. Success is about broken lives that start to be mended, bridges built to people prepared to ask questions and progressive growth to be like Jesus Christ.

The reality is that larger churches often have their own particular problems but they are better at disguising them. To be large is not necessarily to be spiritually healthy. Complacency, pride, insularity, prayerlessness and a lack of true dependency on God are not uncommon. Small churches also have their problems, but many comment on the depth of fellowship that is evident. They are places where everyone has a name and if you are missing someone is likely to notice.

Those involved in small rural churches live out their faith in a more local context that permits incarnational models of evangelism to develop. A stronger link is established between the routines of daily life and Sunday worship. There are some ministers who have the privilege of knowing almost all the residents in their village.

Good news for small churches

German church growth researchers Christoph Schalk and Christian A Schwarz surveyed over 1,000 churches in 32 countries on all five continents. Although reporting in general terms, they discovered:

- Small churches with an average of 50 members are 16 times as effective as large churches at winning new members.

- The greatest growth proportionately occurs in churches of less than 100 members. Two 200-member churches generally win twice as many people for Jesus as a single 400-member church.

- The best evangelistic strategy is the co-operation of large and small churches with the aim of multiplying mostly small churches with a balanced measure of quality and quantity.

Source: Christian A Schwarz, *Natural Church Development*, Church-Smart Resources

A small church cannot attempt to do all that a larger church attempts to do. However some have been known to try. Rather than dwell on what your church cannot be or do, it is better to work out what the Lord wants you to do with the resources he has made available. This takes the pressure off and allows the small church to seek excellence in a small number of areas.

> 'The man who lives in a small community lives in a much larger world. The reason is obvious. In a large community we can choose our companions. In a small community our companions are chosen for us.'
>
> **G K Chesterton**

Present opportunities, not past success or failure

What causes a church to settle into past-directed thinking is not so much present difficulty as past success. A church lifts the burden of past success or failure when it focuses instead on present opportunities. What is God calling us to do and how has he equipped us for the challenges of today?

Assess the resources available

Start by asking, 'What are the existing strengths of the church?' These are likely to be linked to the gifts and interests of those presently involved. I can think of churches where people are gifted to work among children or provide meals for the elderly. Others may be strong in practical caring while some have particular gifts for work among men or women. Creative gifts may be used in a variety of ways. If a church is strong in working with adults but without a Sunday School, the outreach to adults must be developed leaving the Sunday School until later.

Other people are good at building relationships, welcoming visitors, offering hospitality and including them in existing groups. They need to be encouraged to use their gifts and not be pressurised into areas for which they are not equipped.

Those who possess particular God-given gifts do not find it a struggle to use them. Their ministries are marked by a joyful enthusiasm and are not a burden. When people work out of a wrong sense of duty and in areas of church life for which they have not been equipped, fatigue and frustration quickly follow.

Younger willing Christians can find their spiritual energy sapped if older and more established people seek to maintain patterns of church life or activities that were developed at times of more settled and predictable attendance patterns.

New life is often breathed into older churches as we sensitively mark what God has previously blessed and then ask what should be the present priorities? The reality is that change is constantly with us. Whenever people join or leave a particular church, the mix of gifts alters.

Do not attempt too much

Every good idea for a new activity can quickly become someone else's responsibility. Those who are quick to say 'Why don't we?' are not always those prepared to do the work. The small or new church requires a very concentrated focus if exhaustion is to be avoided.

Summary

The third lesson concerning faith in the countryside is to concentrate on your strengths not your weaknesses. This will require developing present opportunities, not dwelling on past success or failure; assessing the resources available and not attempting to do too much.

Activity One
Quality Control exercise

1. What is your church particularly good at doing?
2. Why do people attend your church?
3. What do you do that no one else in your community is doing?
4. What services do you provide that many do not?
5. What ministries do you offer that you don't have the talents, gifts, or abilities to do well?
6. Select one aspect of your church life and share ideas on how it could be better, using the resources and people you already have.

Activity Two
Unearthing the buried talents

> This is an exercise ideal for use first by church leaders who then go on and lead a small group. Seek to include as many people as possible and you may discover some surprising results. Quite often people are willing to use their gifts, but have never been asked.

1. If you could go back in a time machine with thousands of pounds worth of gold coins and knowledge that you have gained about the events leading up to the present year, how would you invest the money and then come back to get a return on your investment?
2. Read the parable of the talents in Matthew 25:14-30.
3. Who do the master and servants represent?
4. Why do you think the Lord adds the phrase 'each according to his ability' in verse 15?
5. Share an instance of how you felt when you used a gift or talent that God had given.
6. Why do you think the master became angry with the servant who hid his talent?
7. How does the reward compare with what was entrusted (verses 19-23)?
8. We all function best as a 'round peg in a round hole.' Are you using the gifts God has given you or are some buried in the ground?
9. How could operating with the gifts and resources that God has clearly given, shape what your church could do? Conversely, how could this help you to feel less frustrated by what you cannot do?

4. No church is a lost cause but change is never easy

Where are you heading?

'Not a lot changes in this village and we want to keep it that way.'
'We tried that once and it didn't work.'

'This is the way we've always done it.'

Most church leaders will have heard such statements, particularly if they try to change anything. Moses faced a storm of protest when the going got tough for Israel in the desert. For many, the perceived dangers ahead were too challenging. Morale had been sapped through constant complaint and retreating seemed more attractive than continuing.

'That night all the people of the community raised their voices and wept aloud. All the Israelites grumbled against Moses and Aaron, and the whole assembly said to them, "If only we had died in Egypt! Or in this desert." And they said to each other, "We should choose a leader and go back to Egypt"' (Numbers 14:1,2,4).

Moses had to deal not only with their complaints about him but also with the fact that deep down they were not trusting God for their future. The consequence for this generation which had experienced God's remarkable grace was they would not make it to the Promised Land. They would have preferred to retreat. After 38 years of holding worship services in the desert, nothing happened to advance the purpose of God. Content with simply being sponges soaking up God's blessing, they were unwilling to follow the purposes of God whatever the cost.

Counting numbers can be deceptive

Rural church buildings were often enlarged to accentuate the difference in wealth and status between villages. Seating was sometimes increased in the hope that people would come. They rarely did. A 1901 survey of 14 Northumberland parishes found 13,409 seats in churches and chapels but a population of only 10,970. The survey indicated that only 22% of the church seats were occupied on Sundays.

Throughout the United Kingdom there are faithful committed people who have maintained Christian witness in villages for a long period. They are to be honoured and respected for their dedication and sacrificial service. With the passing of time the work may have become more difficult, new people have not joined and the future is uncertain. Within Rural Ministries, we do not believe any church is a lost cause before a thorough assessment of the present situation and anticipation of the future has taken place. A starting point is to ask, 'What will this church look like in five and ten years' time?' Where the necessity of change is accepted and early advice is sought, we are aware of churches that have been renewed and started to grow.

Definition of insanity

'Doing the same thing over and over and expecting different results.'

Albert Einstein

Much has already been written on the importance of carefully managing change. You may now find it helpful to reflect on how two very different churches have been through some major changes. Each one not only managed to survive but today has a much brighter future.

Rural churches and the Internet

The Internet has come to stay and the Church must continually be exploring how to use it to serve mission especially in isolated areas. Even if you find the Internet intimidating there are probably people in your church or locality who could develop some of the ideas below.

Create a church website

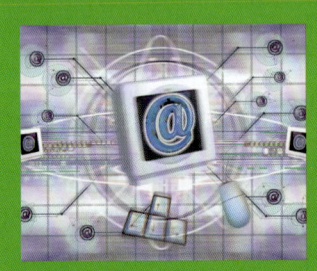

This is not difficult and it does not need to be expensive. Keep it simple. If possible provide access to sermons that are recorded and then available for download. Include stories and material of local interest. Ensure you include map and contact details. Remember many of those moving to a new area will look for churches by using an Internet search engine. If you are not present they may not find you. More than 43,000 UK churches are listed at www.findachurch.co.uk

Use eNewsletters to communicate with people and remember to provide copies for those who do not use the Internet. A website and eNewsletter are among the most time-effective and cost-effective ways of communicating. Consider issues of confidentiality, and any personal, sensitive material should not be included without permission.

Develop a presence on a social networking site if someone will devote the time to updating regularly. These online communities are not a replacement to traditional physical congregations, but a supplement. The time will come when it is appropriate to invite people to meet. Christianity was never designed to be a solitary affair, belonging together in order to learn, grow and serve are important values.

Maintain the personal touch

Simon Bowkett is seeking to establish a contemporary and accessible church at Llandeilo in the heart of Wales. He describes himself as the confessed antithesis of a computer expert and he does not find using computers natural or easy. However, Simon sees making good use of the Internet as important in developing and maintaining contact with those living in isolated places.

The church website already includes audio sermons and short videos providing answers to basic questions. To encourage people to read the Bible, Simon is developing a Good Book Club. Daily Bible reading notes are available and these are discussed in weekly home groups. He aims to increase the number of groups meeting in more remote communities. Small home meetings were very influential in Wales at times when the Christian faith spread rapidly.

As part of the 'Breakout' satellite youth work, a dedicated page has been created on Facebook. This enables effective communication among younger people who now tend to make little use of emails.

Simon is convinced that the Internet serves to supplement the vital personal contact through his work as Rural Chaplain and regular visitation. He takes every opportunity to point people towards the website. Those living in isolated areas are unlikely to use resources on the Internet before they can answer the question, 'Do I know these people?'

For further information see
www.grace-llandeilo.org.uk

Simon Bowkett at home on his farm

Cul-de-sac or road to growth?

This is the story of what is happening to what was an almost derelict parish. In September 2001, Rev Ken Hobbs was appointed as the new Vicar on a House for Duty basis. This means living in the church house with expenses paid but no salary, in return for Sundays and two days a week. Until recently, Ken has continued teaching on a part-time basis at a school 20 miles away. Here is his account of a church transformed.

Albury Parish Church

What greeted me

Albury is a village located in the depths of rural Surrey. It has a scattered population of approximately 1,000 adults. They are a mix of older village families and the more recent arrivals who have opted for a rural lifestyle.

I quickly discovered that the average age of the church congregation was over 70 and numbered less than 20 with the majority coming from the older village families. The church was effectively disconnected from both ordinary village people and two new generations. As far as churchmanship was concerned, they were more low than high but suffered in my view by being neither. There is nothing worse than a dead low church! The church was highly conservative and modern Christian music was almost unheard of and would certainly be disliked.

What became immediately apparent was that the church was in terminal decline. My near wilderness church garden came to serve as a parable of the parish and what can be done with unpromising ground. Both my garden and the church have been transformed.

Ground preparation

Early days were far from easy. The tiny congregation arrived without speaking and left as soon as the blessing was pronounced. A number of the older people found my simple style of conducting worship and preaching from the Bible decidedly uncomfortable. Some left for pastures new or no pastures at all. One lady announced to the village that I had 'taken God out of the church.'

Ground preparation is hard work and takes time. Discouragement set in. There were no services appropriate for young people or families. The music and the worship were dire. There was only a lectern Bible in the church. Internal and external communications were non-existent and the only thing you would consider inviting anyone to was a jumble sale and the Christmas Fair! Even the notion of having coffee after a church service appeared to be a novel idea.

Bring in the Ground Force team

I discovered that in the past some godly people had been praying for and working in the area. A lay leader from a nearby town had run a small toddler service. In the late 1990s, an Alpha Course commenced. Following the course those involved continued to meet twice monthly in the Albury Bible Study Group. Equally important was the prayer and practical support received from my wife Margaret and friends in our old parish. Some were prepared to regularly travel to support us and swell the congregation.

Gradually we introduced the church to the idea of change. 'How to get a grip on the future without losing touch with the past' is a book title that described the task of engaging the two lost generations in the village without alienating the older members of the congregation.

'The most bewildering, gut-wrenching, bowel-opening, faith-stretching, water-walking experience was discovering where and how to start. All the success stories of church growth seemed to be earthed in urban or third world contexts. We felt overwhelmed with the size of the task.'

Ken Hobbs

A growing harvest

In the early months, we did a few simple practical things like putting Bibles in the pews; removing the old hymnbooks and standardising service times.

While initially maintaining the more traditional Communion service, a significant change was introducing twice-monthly all-age worship. This is an adult service that includes children and not a children's service that adults have to endure. These services are simple, lively and welcoming. They are not wacky and off the wall!

At the first service, 4 families came – 8 adults and 11 children almost exclusively from within the parish. As others started to join them, we discovered that 60% of this congregation had not been regular churchgoers before.

We have placed the teaching of Scripture as the Word of God as the centrepiece of our preaching. We promote Bible reading, give away Bible notes and put our sermons on tape and the church's website. Service books have been re-written in line with Common Worship. We have introduced by a process of creep, a mix of contemporary and traditional music.

A most significant change was moving from the solo ministry to form a shared ministry team. We have been able to include Ministerial Assistants and two interns who have gained parish experience before offering for ordination and commencing their training.

Small groups are the lifeblood of growing churches. Building on the existing Albury Bible Study Group, we have added four other adult groups meeting at different times and locations. Including the children's Sunday groups and clubs, we now have 16 groups meeting in the parish each month which are linked to the church.

Physical changes in the church building include a kitchen, a disabled toilet, a carpeted welcome area including the removal of rear pews, a sound system, a new driveway with disabled parking, and exterior lighting. Plans are well advanced for a large side extension to create a church lounge and teaching space.

As much as possible, we have concentrated on community participation and involvement. I am seen a lot around the village and at events, with or without a dog collar.

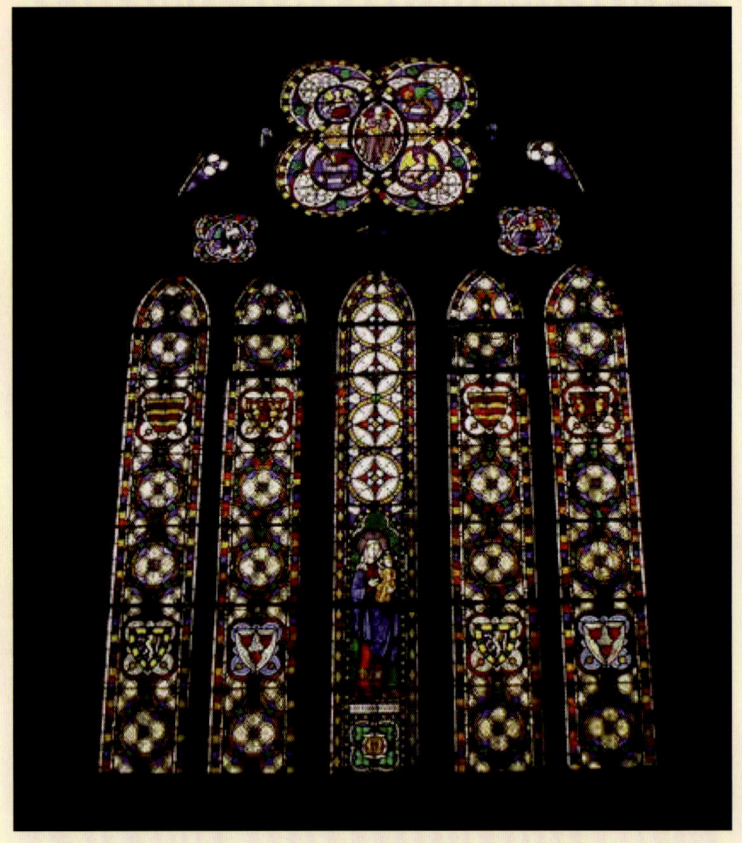

The Ancient church of St Peter and St Paul, Albury Estate, Albury, Surrey

Climate change

There was recognition on the part of the majority of the older members of the congregation that things had to change. They were in the last chance saloon and they knew it. We now have as many as 120 people attending all-age worship services. Our current estimate is that we are in touch with 20% of the parish and on many Sundays around 10% of the parish are in church. The funeral ministry in a village is another vital and influential part of our work.

With growth, new challenges emerge. How do we introduce our increasing number of teenagers to big church life in town, yet retaining youth cells and service opportunities in the parish? How do people move from being attendees to become serious Christian disciples who are not consumers, but providers? A growing church requires more than two days' unpaid work from the Vicar. What will be the future pattern of ministry in the parish? And how do we prepare for my forthcoming retirement?

Our experience at Albury is not unique. But it is relatively uncommon for a small village to experience such a developing spiritual harvest. We do not have a monopoly of spiritual vision, growth and enterprise. Mistakes have been made and we have fallen into the trap of transferring big church thinking into a small church context.

As I reflect on what God has done, I am convinced that there are dozens of potential clergy and lay leaders with underused or unlocked gifts, lurking in the pews of large churches. If released, they could make a life-changing spiritual difference to village communities. There are people more pagan and in spiritual need than in the African bush where we began our Christian ministry a generation ago. Rural churches do not have to be heading down a cul-de-sac, and there is a road to growth.

Ken and Margaret Hobbs
www.alburychurches.org

Flowers in the desert

Fenlands Church, Tydd Gote, Wisbech, Cambridgeshire

Some people laugh when they hear the name of the village where our work is centred. A 'gote' is not an animal but a channel of water. It was no laughing matter in 2004 when the church was about to close down. Church attendance relied on a faithful few and these struggled against negative attitudes and spiritual opposition. However, the place had a history of faithful, praying people who believed that God had a work to do in the Fenlands!

Nene Family Church, part of the Newfrontiers family of churches in Peterborough, had a long-standing association with the fellowship at Tydd Gote. Rural Ministries leaders called for a review in Tydd Gote and David Chapman, the lead elder at the Peterborough church was asked to attend, along with other interested parties. At this meeting David offered to bring a team from the Peterborough church, 30 miles away, to restart the work. There was faith that God still wanted to do something in the area and make Jesus' name famous there.

The offer was accepted and the process of 're-planting' the church began. The few that remained of the previous fellowship found it very difficult to adjust, but most did – eventually. During the first year there was little growth, but time was spent in establishing the foundations and beginning effective local outreach.

After the first year, the team from Peterborough began to hear the call to move to the area. One couple moved into the property owned by the church. Dave and Jenny Chapman took the bold step to move into nearby Sutton Bridge. Others in the team who had helped with worship and teaching gradually reduced their commitment. New leadership was emerging as people started attending from the area. Our first baptism was a great time for celebration.

There were several deaths during the first years. We seemed to be holding funeral services on a regular basis. Yet, this resulted in newcomers joining us – in particular a family with a Christian background whose grief at the death of a patriarchal grandfather led them to renewed faith in the Lord Jesus Christ. Also, we received gifts from the legacies of some who had good memories of fellowship at Tydd Gote.

Things progressed. We grew in numbers slowly but surely and were able to sustain numerous outreach events and start a Sunday Morning Family Service. We introduced film nights, barbecues and open-air music, using a mix of secular and sacred music in outreach. We want to go to where the people are and, when they are invited into our buildings, we want a welcoming atmosphere that avoids too much of a religious shock! So we have drama sketches, puppets, a coffee shop, a mums and toddlers group and film nights and clubs for children. Alongside these we worked with the Village Committee and made our buildings available for their use.

We might have 'little strength', but this does not mean that we have none. Therefore we have ploughed, sown and reaped. Initially when some asked for baptism, we took everyone down to the supporting church in Peterborough. This was a great joy – especially baptising a lady in her eighties. We love to see her worshipping the Lord will her whole being! The people at Nene Family Church saw the results of their faith in sending out a team as they welcomed all the new folk who had joined us in Tydd Gote.

Our character as a rural church has changed a great deal from the days before 2004. Some miss the 'old hymns' or the more formal kind of service. However, our approach has been to make church accessible to all and to extend our work beyond the 80 people who live in the village. While we enjoy more contemporary lighting, music, drama and puppets, the basics of prayer, worshipping God, and Bible teaching are there in full view. As new people join us we are looking at church planting in two other places in this part of the Fenlands.

The chapel at Tydd Gote faced closure. The congregation was numbered in single figures. There were no families or children attending. All this has changed through the grace of God. Tydd Gote Chapel, now known as Fenlands Church, is open daytime and evenings, weekdays and weekends. People come and go to our coffee shop, join our music group, attend our Alpha Course, meet together at our mums and toddlers group and engage in all kinds of activities. On Sundays, the building feels full when we meet and faith, hope and love are alive here. We have young families and a few teens attending. A new start has been made and strong foundations are being established for the future.

As Isaiah 35:1 says, 'The desert and the parched land will be glad; the wilderness will rejoice and blossom. Like the crocus…'

David Chapman

www.fenlandschurch.co.uk

Summary

The fourth lesson concerning faith in the countryside is that no church is a lost cause, but change is never easy. Concentrating on the most important areas is where you begin.

Activity One

Change-making for beginners

As a way of preparing for something new, explore answers to some of the questions below.

1. Think of a major change you personally experienced in the past five years. What was your initial reaction to the thought of that change? What helped you get through it? Did it turn out to be a good thing?

2. When was the last time your church made an important change? What was the result?

3. What changes should churches not consider making?

4. What are some signs that a church is not ready for a change?

5. If leaders are to introduce some significant changes how should they go about it? Think about the importance of necessary preparations; a suitable time frame; seeking permission to attempt something new for a short period of time, and how to evaluate any change.

6. What kinds of changes could you make to better fulfil our mission?

Activity Two

Where are we now?

Every church is at some point on this life cycle:

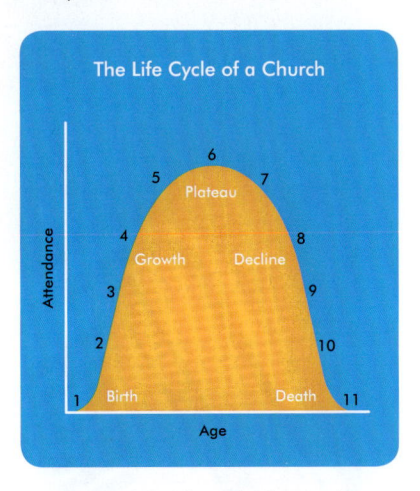

The Life Cycle of a Church

(Attendance vs Age: 1 Birth, 2, 3, 4 Growth, 5, 6 Plateau, 7, 8 Decline, 9, 10, 11 Death)

Source: Developed from Charles Handy, *The Empty Raincoat: Making Sense of the Future*, Random House, 1995

Your task is to discover where your church fits on this simplified pattern of what happens in many churches. Circle the number that corresponds to where you would place the church at the present time. Compare your answers with others and work out the average number for those participating. The average figure will be the group's estimate of whether the church is growing, in a plateau, or declining.

Discuss together what you have discovered and the future implications.

Activity Three
Unchanging priorities

Healthy churches, whatever the tradition to which they belong, are involved in at least six basic functions:

1. Worship
2. Outreach/Witness
3. Nurture/Discipleship
4. Ministry
5. Fellowship
6. Mission

These functions overlap but all are required. When a church overemphasises one to the detriment of others it is in danger of imbalance and losing its way. Take a look at your own church and ask:

1. Which of the six functions do you recognise?
2. What priority does each one receive?
3. What is currently receiving the lowest priority?
4. How could you redress any imbalance?

Activity Four
What future for your church?

Circle YES or NO for each question.

1. Is there a Sunday attendance of more than 20? YES NO
2. Is there a reasonable spread of ages? YES NO
3. Does our regular income exceed expenditure? YES NO
4. Are we prepared for necessary future major expenditure? YES NO
5. Is more than 10% of church income spent on outreach to the local community? YES NO
6. Are there at least two competent leaders? YES NO
7. Does the church have a good reputation locally? YES NO
8. Have there been signs of growth over the past 10 years? YES NO
9. Does our church demonstrate a healthy spiritual life? YES NO
10. Have the majority of members been associated with the church for more than 20 years? YES NO
11. Do people talk more about the future than the past? YES NO
12. Have you sought help? YES NO
13. Do people believe that restoration and growth are God's plan? YES NO

5. Make buildings work for maximum benefit

Buildings – a blessing or a curse?

Many new churches meet in borrowed buildings. Such churches are often effective in reaching those who would never attend a traditional church building. The downside is that there are also people who expect if they attend a church that it should *look* like a church. The disadvantages of not having your own building often surface for the new church. With any increase in people attending there are new opportunities for daytime and evening activities. The time and commitment required to set up and take down the necessary arrangements for Sunday worship and midweek activities can be considerable, as can the ongoing cost of room-hire.

Desire for a church to own a building has led some to purchase unsuitable properties without adequate professional advice, which prove expensive to maintain. This tends to divert money that was previously used for ministry into maintenance.

The reality is that many church buildings in the countryside are only used for two or three hours each week. Vandalism, dry rot, insect infestation and leaking roofs are among a long list of potential curses for any established church building. Few would like to calculate the annual cost of this provision for a small number of people. The resource currently being used may have been provided by a rich benefactor or by previous generations when patterns of church attendance and worship were very different. Asking how buildings may effectively serve both the church and wider community encourages the present generation to make a lasting contribution. They too may be involved in leaving a valuable legacy to future generations.

Adaptation not fossilisation

Sensitive adaptation, underpinned by understanding of the existing buildings allows a greater range of uses. One of the major changes in the past twenty years has been churches prepared to open their doors not only for worship but gatherings of the local community. This is not a novel idea.

Originally, many churches did not contain pews and would have consisted of an open flexible space.

Until the building of community and village halls, churches were the only buildings large enough to host community events. Records show that parish churches hosted meetings, debates, elections and legal proceedings, as well as festivities. They could also house the library and the school, store any fire-fighting equipment, act as the local armoury, as well as at times being used as the jail and as a night shelter. In some cases prior to 1849, the church building even provided space for cockfighting!

'Church buildings should be given back to the local community, albeit with safeguards for worship... Change has been the life-blood of the country church through the ages. Adaptation will be more important than preservation.'

Sir Roy Strong, *A Little History of the English Country Church*, Jonathan Cape 2007

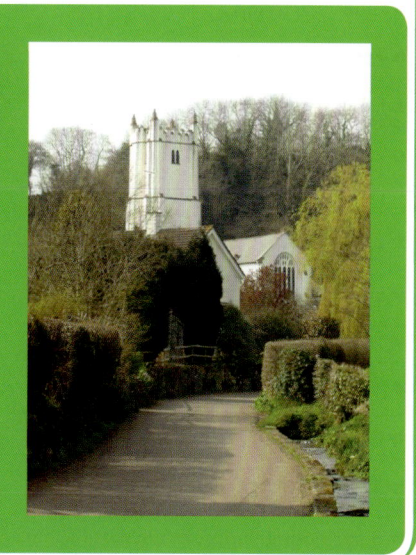

61

Today, churches are being forced to consider ways of using church buildings more effectively – seven days a week instead of just on Sundays. Churches are being brought back into the total life of the village in a way that has not been seen since the Middle Ages.

As well as the more usual purposes for which church buildings are used, I am aware of the following taking place in country churches:

- Local history and art exhibition
- Music and drama
- After-school club
- Country dancing class
- Film club
- Adult education
- Parent and Toddler group
- Lunch club
- Thrift shop providing low cost clothes and furniture
- Craft activities for children and adults
- Coffee shop and meeting point
- Short-mat bowls
- Antenatal and Parenting courses
- Debt counselling
- Back-to-work course
- Basic computing skills course
- Careers advice
- Bereavement counselling
- Marriage and family support
- Venue for school visit
- Post Office

Raising the standards

Paul writes in Colossians 3:23 'Whatever you do, work at it with all your heart, as working for the Lord.' Regrettably when it comes to church buildings, that may easily slip into an 'anything will do' attitude. This contrasts with the much higher expectations that people in the UK now have regarding heating, seating, lighting and audio-visual presentation. One of my most frequent laments is 'Why do many churches serve such appalling coffee?'

Church buildings often give the impression that we should worship God in a time capsule. I deeply appreciate traditional church buildings, especially where prayer has taken place for hundreds of years. It is most encouraging to see churches that have sought appropriate help in order to maintain the traditional character of a building while making it fit for purpose.

Special people – special needs

Surrounding your church are probably more people with special needs than you realise. Are they part of your mission focus? They may never be present because you have not considered their specific needs or made any provision for them. Rather than assume you know their needs, it is better to ask.

Providing suitable access for wheelchairs should be seen as a privilege and not an unnecessary expense. Designated spaces for wheelchair users to sit with friends and be part of the congregation are helpful. Isolation is never appropriate. For some, providing seating with arm support permits those with mobility problems a little extra help when standing. Hearing problems are increasing, and installing an induction loop system is always helpful. Large-print or Braille Bibles and being able to see the words for songs and hymns, especially when projected, should not be assumed.

What could the future look like?

With the breakdown in the provision of social and essential services especially in isolated places, I expect we will increasingly see church buildings used to provide post offices, community shops, doctors' surgeries and even police stations.

Summary

The fifth lesson concerning faith in the countryside is that any buildings must work for the maximum benefit. Higher standards are necessary and provision must be made for people with a variety of disabilities. Maintaining church buildings or other places of worship is not incompatible with other uses.

More than a physical makeover

First impressions make a difference. Buildings, landscaping and signs make a difference. What does it say about our church if paint is chipped and cracked, windows not cleaned, the decoration is antiquated and the signage is not helpful? A message is being communicated, although it is not the message we want to give. We may be a loving church with an incredible vision to reach people, but they may never give us a chance because we did not give attention to our first impressions.

This was very much on my heart when on New Year's Day 2007 we took over the old Mission Hall at Blofield in the north of Norfolk. The building is around 120 years old and in spite of some modernisation 20 years ago, it appeared to be unloved and uncared for, as well as looking its age. When it came to refurbishing the property, I was very clear how the building *was* and *was not* going to look. The plan was to remove as many physical barriers to people coming to church as I could.

The traditional village chapel at Blofield, Norfolk

Hard bench-type pews were replaced by a mix of round banquet tables and chairs. We added stylish, comfy bucket-style armchairs and coffee tables. Now, the interior resembles a conservatory with lots of leafy plants and zoned areas created with open lattice screens. My motivation came from a heart that wants everything we do and have to be excellent. This is what I would expect in my home. Our building is there for the community and it does not belong to any of us. We want to glorify God with it. We serve only the best Fairtrade coffee in china cups, with homemade biscuits and cakes on china plates with pastry forks and good quality serviettes. 'That will do' is a phrase never used within our team.

The transformation completed

I was adamant that we would never hear complaints about our building being cold, so we installed the best heating possible for the job. We must be one of the few churches where people actually ask to have the heating turned down! Plus we wanted us to be known for our plush loos – and we are.

The physical atmosphere of our building has removed a lot of the usual 'church barriers', and our warm, relaxing, friendly environment has played a huge part in our growing relationship with the community in creating a sense of belonging. We run a monthly craft group and also a music+movement group for pre-schoolers. On these occasions, The Rock Café is open for parents to enjoy coffee and homemade cake. We find mothers love to chat and very moving, personal discussions have taken place through the relationships being made.

Our Puppet Service every two months has attracted quite a few families who have been pleasantly surprised when they step foot inside the building. Many times we are asked, 'Are you sure this is a church?'

> We also have a scrapbook/craft group called 'Scrapfest' that meets fortnightly on Fridays and Saturdays. In collaboration with the local playgroup we arrange joint activities including hosting a very successful Ladies Pamper Evening.
>
> Through careful use of space and good design, we now have a very versatile building. Space used by children on a Sunday was easily turned into a plush restaurant setting to serve a three-course meal for the participants at the end of their parenting course. The environment we have created does not limit us. Rather it is proving beneficial for many people who would not normally think of going near a church.
>
> **Rosemarie McDonald, The Rock Church, Blofield, Norfolk**

Activity

Through a different pair of eyes

1. Church buildings create positive and negative impressions. Ask several people, including some who do not attend the church, to take a fresh look at the building. Their task is to look carefully and then share their observations. The same task could be used if you have a church website.

2. Does the area around the building look cared for?

3. The noticeboard is the last thing regular attendees look at and the first thing visitors read. What does it reveal about the church and its priorities?

4. Is the entrance obvious and welcoming?

5. What signage is observable both inside and outside the church? What is missing?

6. What do you notice when you first walk in?

7. What provision is made for people with sight or hearing impairment and other special needs?

8. Does this building look like it is for adults only? What obvious provision is made for children?

9. Are you regularly making the best use of available space?

10. If you had to decide on two immediate priorities, what would they be?

11. When was your home last decorated inside and outside?

6. Church planting needs to be on the agenda

Church planting is not about how many people you can get through the church doors on Sunday morning but about reaching those who are unchurched. Counting numbers is not highly rated as a value among church planters.

Although many are speaking about the importance of church planting, there has been little attention given to the rural context. Barry Osborne of Rural Sunrise, writing in 2004, reported on extensive research he had conducted into rural church planting. He contacted individuals, all main denominations and mission agencies known to work in rural areas in England, Scotland and Wales. He discovered less than 20 new churches with most being in larger villages.

As part of the objectives of Rural Ministries, we are committed to encouraging and supporting church-planting initiatives. There continue to be obstacles to overcome and questions answered regarding why and how to plant churches.

Dealing with objections

Overcoming NIMBG syndrome

Most church leaders would agree that church planting is a good idea so long as it is NIMBG – Not In My Back Garden. In Britain today it is virtually impossible to plant a church without affecting someone else. Competition should be avoided, especially as there are many areas lacking churches clear on the essential truths of the Christian faith and in contact with local people. Where there has been a consistent pattern of death and decline in church life, a missional perspective will consider forming new churches.

When we think territorially and want to be over protective of what we may already have, a new church, or a different expression of church, may appear to be a threat. An existing church may be in contact with only 20% of the local residents. We cannot afford to be complacent or defensive when others attempt to reach the remaining 80%. It is possible to turn Christ's great statement to build his church on its head to make it an expression of our self-centred insecurity: 'I will build *my* church – so don't go building *your* church.' When we pray 'Your kingdom come,' this is a request that there will be more churches capable of reaching beyond existing boundaries. Church planting is always an exercise in kingdom-mindedness.

Do we need more churches when many are struggling?

This is the question I find is most frequently asked. Another is 'Surely with so many churches struggling for their existence, we only spread the resources even more thinly?' While appreciating the questions there is often an underlying assumption that church planting and church restoration are somehow in opposition to each other. Both are important but very different tasks.

The potential of the beautiful bride of Christ

'There is nothing like the local church when it's working right. Its beauty is indescribable. Its power is breathtaking. Its potential is unlimited. It comforts the grieving and heals the broken in the context of community. It builds bridges to seekers and offers truth to the confused. It provides resources for those in need and opens its arms to the forgotten, the downtrodden and the disillusioned. It breaks the chains of addictions, frees the oppressed, and offers belonging to the marginalised of this world. Whatever capacity for human suffering, the church has greater capacity for healing and wholeness. **The church has many critics but no rivals.**'

Bill Hybels, *Courageous Leadership*

Why plant churches?

Reasons for church planting are found in the New Testament and are supported by practical considerations.

Jesus intended churches to be planted. He made a momentous statement when he promised to build his church (Matthew 16:18). He spoke at a time when the storm clouds were gathering as his death was imminent. Neither the circumstances that surrounded him nor even death itself would hinder his plans. His disciples were scattered through the Roman Empire taking the gospel with them. As they preached that gospel, churches were planted.

Evangelism will always lead to church and the church is Jesus' programme. We co-operate with the purposes of God as new churches are established. He is committed to seeing churches established and growing. In church history, every major movement of the Holy Spirit has resulted in churches being planted.

The Great Commission requires churches to be planted

As disciples are made in all nations they are to be baptised and taught (Matthew 28:19). Baptism was to be a sign of belonging to a new community where people would learn obedience to Christ. The spread of the Christian faith required new disciples, not just converts, being made and incorporated into a growing number of churches.

> 'The single most effective evangelistic methodology under heaven is planting new churches.'
> Peter Wagner,
> *Church Planting for a Greater Harvest*

The book of Acts illustrates a church planting movement

In Luke's second book, he tells of the continuing work of Jesus through his church. Acts provides a geographical outline of the spread of Christianity:

- Commencing in Jerusalem (Acts 1:1-8:3)
- Spreading to Judea and Samaria (Acts 8:4-12:25)
- Advancing to the ends of the earth (Acts 13:1-28:31)
- The work continues and we are those involved in Acts 29 and beyond.

Paul's missionary journeys were church planting ventures into predominately pagan cultures. He was an innovator unwilling to maintain the status quo, and he had to deal with considerable opposition from those with established religious mindsets. Paul identified key cities that would not keep the good news of Christ to themselves, but would go on and impact whole regions. Today we need more city and suburban churches to honestly say they have done little to share resources with rural churches in their region.

There is a pattern identifiable in Acts consisting of four crucial elements of church growth.

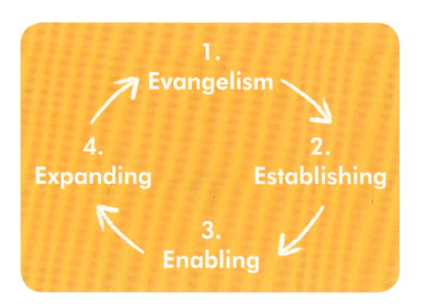

1. Evangelism
2. Establishing
3. Enabling
4. Expanding

The final stage of expansion involves not only a growth in numbers in one place but spreading into new areas to establish churches. When any one of the four elements is not in place, church growth slows and new churches are not established. Where two or more elements receive little attention, the church within a nation is usually in decline.

New churches are more effective in reaching people

With the passage of time, established churches tend to spend more time, energy and resources, on existing members rather than on the unchurched. New churches cannot afford to do so and keep evangelism as a priority.

An usual place of meeting

South African born Siya Twani has been involved in the task of evangelism and church planting in South Woodham Ferrers in Essex. He is particularly concentrating on meeting local people and does not operate from a traditional church base but from a sports club known as Club Woodham. Here he is affectionately known as the 'Peoples' Minister.' One of the fitness instructors at Club Woodham said of Siya, 'He is a big celebrity around here. He is everyone's friend. When I first started here he gave me a blessing. What has really helped is that Siya had belief in me and I recognise that every little bit helps.'

Here, Siya answers questions about his unusual approach to evangelism.

Why are you working out of a sports club?

I have been coming here for six years essentially to keep fit. It is important that I keep fit with my body, mind and spirit. The club is also my mission field. This is the place where I connect with the community. I offer a listening ear, seeking to comfort and support.

What are some of the ways in which you have been able to serve these people?

There are a number of people who are lonely and really appreciate someone to sit down and have a cup of coffee with them. With men I meet in the gym, they would not normally go to church but they open up their hearts to me.

Following the death of a well-known member of the club, I was asked to conduct the funeral service on club premises. I was able to speak to more than 400 people on that one occasion. The service was well received and I have been asked to conduct thanksgiving services for several children as well as a marriage service for two club members.

What is your thinking on church planting?

We want to take church to where people are. At Club Woodham, I have access to the lives of hundreds of people. Some are lost, others are searching and I want to introduce them to Christ. Following that, church may make some sense to them. We are working on a Fit For life programme and a Happy Hour family event with children on either Saturday or Sunday in the late afternoon.

Siya Twani outside Club Woodham, Essex

New churches provide greater leadership development opportunities

Many who never become leaders in established churches, where length of tenure and maintaining the status quo are often important values, find their gifts develop in new churches.

New churches are prepared to cross cultural divides

Church plants can and must seek new ways of being church. The necessities of prayer, faith and sacrificial living come sharply into focus, as they seek to reach people where they are.

New churches can be a blessing to established churches

Church plants can be a catalyst for renewal, promoting healthy motivation for established churches. They are research and development centres for the wider church.

New churches are required to meet the challenges

With an estimated twice as many churches closing than are opened each year, we need hundreds of new churches to reach the unreached people of the United Kingdom. Many of these people live in the countryside. The people we seek to meet in the name of Jesus deserve that we do not take church planting too lightly.

> Possibly there is a better question than 'Why plant churches?' It is, 'Why not?'

A fresh start in the Lake District

The 'Fresh Expressions' initiative to encourage people to establish new and different forms of church for our changing culture has received support from many church leaders. Based on the understanding that many churches have lost touch with people, there is the opportunity to develop more simple patterns of church life.

Following a short period leading the Rural Ministries partner church in Bawtry, South Yorkshire, John and Sue Sainsbury moved to Witherslack in Cumbria. Their desire was to fulfil a long-held calling to establish what they call 'Outreach House.' Here they describe some of their work:

John and Sue, what are you seeking to do?

Perhaps it's more a question of *who* we're seeking to *be*. We're seeking to live a life that is all about being disciples of Christ. We're passionate about God's church and our intention is that, as we live for Him, we will make disciples of people totally untouched by church as we know it. Outreach House is a centre for missionary activity into a small village community.

What does that look like and what are your plans for the future?

We are living what we call a 'rhythm of life' that puts God at the centre of all that we do. For seven years we are committed to grow as disciples through praying together, progressively studying a chapter of the Bible every morning, working locally and opening the House for community activities in the evenings. Every bit of the day is spent putting our knowledge of God into practice. Our fellow team-members are fully involved in the local community. Our hope is that as we live like this we will find others drawn to Jesus and this will be the foundation of a discipleship-orientated church that God can use to transform lives and our whole community.

How are you going about establishing relationships?

Slowly but surely we are building real friendships. One of our key objectives is to be *in* the community for the community and everything we do is with the hope of introducing people to Jesus. So, rather than 'telling' people what they need, we work to meet the needs they know themselves to have and serve them as well as we can.

One important step was to work towards reopening the village shop and post office. The Outreach House team spearheaded this campaign. Boosted by £30,000 raised from £10 shares sold to local people, a total of over £100,000 was pledged from fundraising, shares and public funds. An ambitious concept became an unstoppable challenge, and the shop is thriving. The shop goes way beyond being a place to buy things. We wanted somewhere for people to meet, talk and find a kind smile.

Team member Maria Garner manages the shop volunteers and she says, 'One of our aims here is "to be in the community, and for the community." As we work together, many meaningful friendships are being formed. The warm welcome and a place to sit and chat are particularly well received. I praise God for this genuine reason to daily connect with so many from the village and we pray that ultimately some will connect with our Lord God.'

The village shop reopens

Another significant development has been a group of church and local people to help HEAL Africa, a grass-roots organisation in Goma on the Rwandan border of the Democratic Republic of Congo. The team and community have raised an incredible £20,000. We've been overwhelmed by just how involved and enthusiastic the whole community has been. I think in the Christian world, we tend to forget just how wild and counter-intuitive for many people it is to go to dangerous places and pour ourselves out for the love of Jesus. The impact on our little Lakeland community of sending ordinary folk has been surprising and inspiring.

What are you hoping for at the end of seven years?

We will have completed the study of the whole Bible and established a learning community of practising disciples. We have made a start and others are starting to join us. As we read the Bible, we cannot but be radicalised and challenged to the very depths of who we are.

Our prayer is that a solid church, a small outpost of the Kingdom of God, will have been established with its own local leaders, ready to plant into another village. There has already been a massive positive impact on our local community — far more than we have ever experienced in any other church of which we have been part. It does feel we're truly incarnated here.

John and Sue Sainsbury, Outreach House, Witherslack, Cumbria

www.outreach-house.org

How to plant churches

As well as supporting existing churches, Rural Ministries is currently assisting eight new churches and mission projects in the countryside. Each one is fragile and the challenges are enormous. We are learning quickly about some of the joys and challenges in the unpredictable adventure of church planting.

To those churches seeking to plant, and others prepared to venture forth as church-planting missionaries in the United Kingdom, we would advise:

Count the cost

This comes first. Jesus warned of the dangers of enthusiastically commencing projects without considering all that may be involved (Luke 14:28-33). Church planting requires careful preparation and is always costly. There will be opposition to face, discomfort to endure and regular faith-stretching moments.

Where an existing church is prepared to release people to form a new church, it is always costly. Seeing people leave is often particularly difficult for existing church leaders who understand church growth as growing more people in one place. Without sacrifice, church planting is impossible.

Ideally someone will be available to lead the new church on a part-time or full-time basis. Additional costs may include venue hire, equipment and publicity, and a realistic budget is required. The good news is that there is a blessing that comes to churches which give (Acts 20:35). We are observing that where churches support others there is clear evidence of growth taking place in both the existing and the new church.

> 'The plans of the diligent lead to profit as surely as haste leads to poverty.'
> Proverbs 21:5

Identify the motives

People start churches for many reasons and with a range of differing motives. Church planting is only helpful if it enables us to participate more fully in the mission of God. He is interested in more people becoming disciples, prodigal Christians returning and existing Christians developing and growing.

Start developing leaders – now

If an existing church is considering planting and waits to discover surplus leaders, it is unlikely to ever start new churches. All churches need more leaders, children's workers, musicians, preachers, youth workers, administrators, small group leaders and so on. Wise leaders will make it a priority to grow leaders for both their current and future work.

Avoid being married to a model

It is possible to read books or attend conferences and be attracted to a model that has been effective elsewhere. Some principles may be transferable, but each place and group of people is unique. A willingness to experiment and be flexible is essential. Overseas missionaries are constantly asking 'Who? When? Where?' of their local context. Taking time to appreciate the particular history and stories within an area are important starting points. What can help is learning from those who have planted churches and do not hide their battle scars. They have much to share regarding their mistakes, failures, and successes.

Church planting models and dangers

1. **Runners.** This is the strawberry plant model. There are close ties to the original where resources are made available in the early stages. There is danger that the new plant may end up being a similar expression of the original church for either good or bad. Strawberry runners are very good for producing strawberries but not so good for runner beans.

2. **Grafts.** Here a new shoot is attached to an old stalk in order to bring a restoration of health. There needs to be an acceptance of new leaders and potentially painful change. The past cannot be perpetuated. Remember the parable of the wine and wineskins in Mark 2:22.

3. **Transplants.** Agree to divide and send people to establish a new work or revive a tired work. There is a danger of quickly becoming occupied with people's own needs rather than making disciples.

4. **Seed.** This may be blown a considerable distance and drop, supported by individuals in different places. There is the risk of isolation. Therefore Jesus sent his disciples out in pairs, and Paul established teams.

Clarify the focus

Without clarity, the new church can exhaust itself by running in too many directions or attempting to please everyone. The following questions start to define:

Beliefs
What are the foundations?

Vision
What could this church look like in the future?

Mission
What has God called and equipped you to do?

Values
What is really important to you?

Strategy
What are we going to do and when?

Answering these questions and producing a short written summary will help you deal with two types of people likely to appear in a new church. There will be those prepared and sent by God, and others prepared by the enemy to spread discontent or hijack the plant. Church plants struggle when they are too all-embracing and fail to confront the disruptive.

Invest in partnerships

No longer can we work in isolated units. The New Testament assumes there will be some sort of relationship between churches. We are not in opposition with each other and consultation with existing leaders in an area is essential in attempting to avoid misunderstandings. We are discovering that there is a common characteristic in healthy rural churches and church plants. They resist a 'go it alone' mindset. Our strongest rural church plants are well supported by churches and individuals elsewhere.

Is this church planting or replanting?

Steve Bell is Minister of Beulah Evangelical Church situated in a seaside village on the Isle of Wight. Here he answers questions about his approach to establishing a church and the link with Rev James Leggett, Minister at St James Church of England in nearby Ryde.

Steve Bell (left) and **James Leggett**.

What were two major challenges you faced on arrival in 2006?

I inherited a church building that had been there for over 150 years. The elderly congregation had become so small that it was on the brink of closing its doors. There was no leadership structure and the church was in need of re-planting. Ideally I would have liked to have a church planting team, with perhaps two or three families, but this was not possible.

The first challenge was to encourage people to resist the temptation to travel in order to find bigger churches with extensive programmes. We prayed for just a few Christians to join us who would be pioneers of the gospel in their own communities, rather than Christian commuters or consumers.

The other big challenge was how to reach people. Around 80% of the surrounding homes are holiday properties. The resident population consists of a sizeable retired community and some young families. Sadly many did not know of our existence. For our first outreach event we printed and distributed 1,000 flyers and posters, but no new people came.

We needed to commence the patient task of building relationships and getting ourselves known. There was always the temptation to do too much and burn out the few resources we did have.

What plans did you make?

We started by training and equipping those involved in the church to share their faith with their friends. We used the 'Two Ways To Live' course to help us with this. This is available from The Good Book Company (www.thegoodbook.co.uk).

From that foundation we began running a café at village fairs and local events. This combined refreshments with Christian activities for children, literature and meeting people. We commenced a regular series of guest services followed by a free lunch together. We call them 'Real Food Sundays'. Starting with a contemporary theme or question that people might have about Christianity, we explore this in a short presentation and through discussion over lunch.

Contact with the local school has been most helpful. My wife took a part-time job there and I take assemblies and serve on the Board of Governors. One class has come and visited the church.

Help from outside has been invaluable in becoming known, and we have benefited in our outreach activities from visiting mission teams from a couple of theological colleges. Through our partnership with St James Church in Ryde we have been able to benefit from their outreach and youth programmes.

How does the partnership St James in Ryde work in practice?

St James is not a large or a wealthy congregation, but they do want to take God-given opportunities. The foundation of our partnership is the sharing of core convictions about the gospel and a focus on the same things. Some people from St James have been prepared to assist and others have joined us. We have received help with preaching and from the music team.

Church planting and restoration is often lonely. Personally, I benefit from the enriching fellowship, accountability and support that have been available. My children have found friendships and have been able to participate in an excellent youth programme that we could not provide.

It is unlikely that the replanting work at Seaview would have been viable without the support of St James, Ryde.

What progress has been made during the past three years?

Since the re-planting work began there has been a doubling in the congregation size (not difficult when you are small!) and in the age spread of the church family. That now includes children and families. Growth in discipleship has also been evident. A move from a 'maintenance mindset' to 'mission mindset' has been a thrill to see.

What are your hopes for the future?

The growth in the last three years has resulted in a new problem. We are starting to outgrow our church premises. Rather than simply relocate, our vision is to 're-plant' again into a neighbouring community. Discussions are already underway and we look forward to commencing a second church restoration project.

Seaview, Isle of Wight

> We are learning the huge advantages of 'small church' for growing mission-minded disciples of the Lord Jesus in scattered rural and semi-rural communities. Growing a network of interdependent churches seems crucial to long term viability. We seek to grow to a position where the work is sustainable without outside help. We value and will continue to develop the wider network of praying and giving 'friends' who support the work from afar. Working together is the way ahead.
>
> For further information see **www.beulahchurch.co.uk** and **www.stjamesryde.com**

An over-emphasis on independence can obscure the interdependent nature of churches in the New Testament. Fellowship in the gospel was a joy shared in more than one geographical location (Philippians 1:5). This enabled churches to go on and plant more churches.

Time spent developing a wide network of friends and supporters is priceless. I am aware of one urban church plant that has developed a network of more than 300 'Friends' who regularly receive news and prayer updates. Their prayer and practical support is invaluable.

The reality is that not all individuals or churches are in a position to be actively involved in church planting. However, a group of churches working together to identify an area and then share resources may be able to accomplish a great deal.

The fact is that every church had to be planted once. Established churches were once new and there were those who gave sacrificially of time, talents and resources to enable the church to exist. With the Tearfund survey in 2007 indicating that over 32.2 million adults have no connection with church at present, surely we cannot say we already have too many churches and that more are not required.

Summary

Church planting needs to be on the agenda. There are objections that need dealing with patiently but answers may be found when we discover why and how to plant churches.

From the ground up: church planting in Cornwall

The Light and Life network of Free Methodist churches in west Cornwall has been pursuing what they believe to be a God-given vision. This is to see an interconnected church with three 'main centres' of 1,000+ people who live throughout a designated area. Scattered 'congregations' consisting of between 20 and 120 people gather in a local area as a light and witness, seeking to regularly reach the lost for Christ. They are not regarded as 'mini-churches' but 'mission outposts', connected to and resourced by one of the main centres. In each congregation, 'growth groups' for up to 15 people meet regularly for worship, prayer, Bible study, friendship and outreach. When a 'growth group' reaches 15 in number, it is time to begin the process of multiplication.

Built into their understanding of church is that it is designed to 'gather' in order to 'scatter'. As a result, they are rapidly planting new churches. One of the real strengths of this arrangement in a rural area is that it allows people to be part of a large church that finds its expression locally in a series of smaller groups. This is particularly important where parents with children and teenagers are looking for good programmes and a wider circle of friends.

It has to be acknowledged that commencing a cell or network-based church from scratch is much easier than transitioning one that has been in existence for many years. What has been particularly noticeable in this church is the large number of new Christians from often relatively poor backgrounds. These people are breaking new ground.

John Townley moved to Cornwall in 1994 to be minister of the church at Helston. Since then he has been involved in planting congregations in Penzance and Truro. Each location has its own minister, but they all work together contributing to the wider network. All these churches have seen significant numerical growth, with an overall average Sunday attendance of more than 600 people. The latest addition is at Hayle, near St Ives.

TRURO

GROWTH GROUP

CONGREGATION

CENTRAL BOARD

MAIN CENTRE

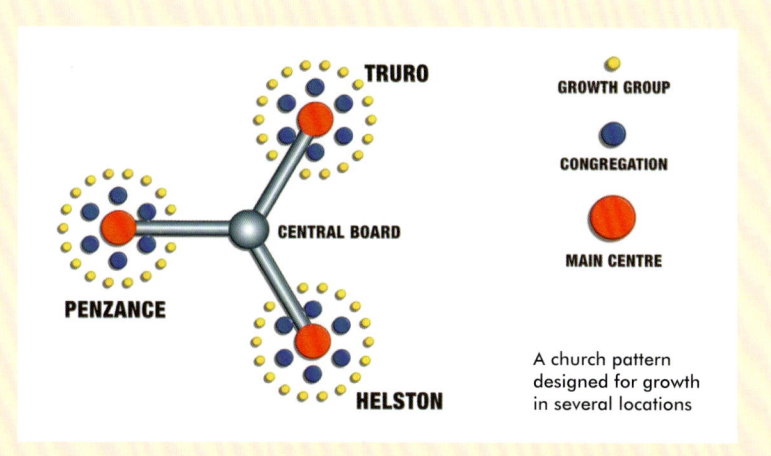

PENZANCE

HELSTON

A church pattern designed for growth in several locations

More recently, John has moved with his wife Becky to establish a new 'main centre' based in St Austell. John took time to meet with other church leaders there to establish good relationships. Some commented 'There are enough people outside the church to go round.'

Starting in September 2008 with a fortnightly prayer meeting in a home, in 2009 they moved to weekly meetings with an average attendance around 20. The first Alpha Course included nine guests, and outreach events are held regularly. Now there are regularly more than 80 people attending Sunday services.

Sustained growth of this kind is rare in the United Kingdom but it does illustrate the potential impact of a church that is prepared to both gather and scatter. Growth is not concentrated in one place and a whole region may benefit.

John Townley leads the Light and Life Free Methodist Church at St Austell, Cornwall

www.lightandlife.co.uk

Activity One

Church planting objections and opportunities

1. What objections have you heard to planting churches? Are they insurmountable problems?
2. How could the parable that Jesus told of the new wine and old wineskins in Matthew 9:17 help with some objections.
3. What qualities are likely to be evident in a church prepared to explore the possibilities of church planting?
4. How would you know if it was the time to plant?
5. What steps would be required if your church was to engage in church planting and who could you ask for help?
6. Complete the sentence: What if the rural church were to …

Activity Two

What does it take to plant a church?

1. In 1 Corinthians 3:6–9, Paul observes, 'The man who plants and the man who waters have one purpose.' What is this purpose?
2. What qualities are required of those who will lead a church plant?
3. What should be the initial priorities of any church plant?
4. At what point could you say a church has been planted?
5. If you cannot find enough leaders who match the high standards agreed above, how will you develop the people you do have?
6. What is your plan to attract new people to your church and keep them?

Endpiece

For those who venture from cities and towns for a visit to the countryside, it is all too easy to develop a superficial understanding of rural areas and their churches. A visit to a stately home or a walk on the hills may suggest an uncomplicated life in a beautifully-preserved environment. A village should contain at least one shop, a traditional pub and church. But in many places, all three have ceased to exist or are in danger of doing so.

Agatha Christie's character Miss Marple and more recently the Vicar of Dibley are stereotypical people you expect to find in a peaceful English village. However, looks can be deceptive. Miss Marple spent most of her life in the small village of St Mary Mead in Downshire and often pointed out **'There is a great deal of wickedness in village life.'**

With the passing of time, both Miss Marple and the Vicar of Dibley are no longer with us and human wickedness increases.

Since the publication of the *Faith in the Countryside* report more than 20 years ago, sadly many country churches have closed. However this is not the complete picture. Increasingly effective are churches confident that in Jesus Christ, we find the enduring source of forgiveness. He brings together a redemptive community to be light in the darkness. His message is relevant at every period of history. Where churches have embraced change, new people are attending. Any rural community should be a better place for all the residents and its whole environment for having a church that demonstrates both the light and life of Christ.

Don't despise the days of small country churches

There are many more examples of healthy rural churches than those included in this publication, but few know of their existence. It is regrettable that church leaders frequently ignore or dismiss the importance of rural areas. They receive a low priority rating. Little attention in many major events is given to including anything appropriate for people in smaller rural churches and examples are nearly always drawn from city contexts. Sadly, talk about the large churches impacting a region is rarely followed by action.

The challenges faced by rural churches are many. Vital to their future will be partnerships with larger churches that are willing to share their resources. Mission is a collective activity and we desperately need to develop mission strategies that not only gather Christians together but also send them out. Urban and suburban churches that have grown by collecting people from smaller churches should appreciate this cannot continue indefinitely. This supply line will cease to exist as more churches close. We must appreciate that where people travel to larger central churches it is largely Christians who do so, leaving others increasingly distant from the Christian message.

Follow the pattern of Jesus Christ

It is not enough to describe cities as the strategic places for mission and fail to follow the example set by the Lord who taught from **village to village**. This pattern continued with the disciples who were sent out two by two. (Mark 6:6,7). To sustain and plant new rural churches it will often require the active involvement of other churches and interested individuals.

There is a great deal that can be done when we follow the example of Jesus who 'went through the towns **and villages**, teaching as he made his way to Jerusalem' (Luke 13:22).

Help is available from Rural Ministries on **(01933) 303050** or use the website **www.ruralministries.org.uk** to contact us. You will also find helpful resources on the website and you may request a free copy of our magazine *Impact*.

Rural Ministries
PLANTING & GROWING RURAL CHURCHES

Resources

The original report of the Archbishop's Commission on Rural Areas was published in 1990 by Churchman Publishing, ISBN/UPC 1850932743. Copies are available on Amazon and Ebay

Jacinta Ashworth, *Churchgoing in the UK*, Tearfund 2007. Copies available on website

George Barna, *The Power of Vision*, Regal Books, 1992

John Benton, *Why Join a Small Church?* Evangelical Press, 2008

Andrew Bowden, *Ministry in the Countryside*, Continuum International Publishing Group, 2003

Peter Brierley, *Vision Building*, Hodder and Stoughton, 1989

Mark Denver, Paul Alexander, *The Deliberate Church*, Crossway, 2005

Leslie J Francis, Keith Littler, Jeremy Martineau, *A Parish Workbook on Lay Ministry in the Country Church*, Canterbury Press, 2000

Sally Gaze, *Mission Shaped and Rural: Growing Churches in the Countryside*, Church House Publishing, 2006

Kevin Harney, *Leadership from the Inside Out*, Zondervan, 2007

Jill Hopkinson, Trevor Wilmott eds, *Re-shaping Rural Ministry*, Canterbury Press, 2009

Bryn Hughes, *Leadership Toolkit*, Kingsway, 2002

Bill Hybels, *Courageous Leadership*, Zondervan, 2002

Norman Ivison, *Expressions the DVD 2*, Church House Publishing, 2007

L Shannon Jung ed, *Rural Ministry – The Shape of the Renewal to Come*, Abingdon Press, 1998

Aubrey Malphurs, *Planting Growing Churches*, Baker, 2003

Jeremy Martineau ed, *Changing Rural Life: A Christian Response to Life and Work in the Countryside*, Canterbury Press, 2004

Marlin Mull, *A Biblical Church Planting Manual: From the Book of Acts*, Wipf and Stock, 2004

Barry Osborne, *Rural Evangelism in the 21st Century*, Grove Books, 2006

David Osborne, *The Country Vicar*, Darton Longman and Todd, 2004

Martin Robinson, *Planting Mission Shaped Churches Today*, Monarch 2006

Alan Smith, *God-shaped Mission: Theological and Practical Perspectives from the Rural Church*, Canterbury Press, 2008

John Stott, *Calling Christian Leaders*, IVP, 2002

Hilary Taylor, *A Toolbox for Small Churches*, Nova Publishing, 2008

Links

Agricultural Christian Fellowship
www.agriculturalchristianfellowship.org.uk

Arthur Rank Centre
www.arthurrankcentre.org.uk

Christian Research
www.christian-research.org.uk

Church Matters – Training and Personal Development
www.church-matters.co.uk

Fellowship for Evangelising Britain's Villages
www.febv.org.uk

Living Leadership – Training and Spiritual Refreshment
www.livingleadership.hostinguk.com

Mission for Christ
www.missionforchrist.org.uk

Rural Evangelism Network
www.ruralmissions.org.uk

Rural Theology Association
www.rural-theology.org.uk

Teal Trust – Leadership Training and Development
www.teal.org.uk